Mediterranean Ninja Foodi Grill Cookbook for Beginners

800-Day Quick & Delicious Ninja Foodi Grill Recipes to Enjoy Your Favorite Mediterranean Meals Easily

Antraw Kaster

© Copyright 2021 Antraw Kaster - All Rights Reserved.

In no way is it legal to reproduce, duplicate, or transmit any part of this document by either electronic means or in printed format. Recording of this publication is strictly prohibited, and any storage of this material is not allowed unless with written permission from the publisher. All rights reserved.

The information provided herein is stated to be truthful and consistent, in that any liability, regarding inattention or otherwise, by any usage or abuse of any policies, processes, or directions contained within is the solitary and complete responsibility of the recipient reader. Under no circumstances will any legal liability or blame be held against the publisher for any reparation, damages, or monetary loss due to the information herein, either directly or indirectly.

Respective authors own all copyrights not held by the publisher.

Legal Notice:

This book is copyright protected. This is only for personal use. You cannot amend, distribute, sell, use, quote or paraphrase any part of the content within this book without the consent of the author or copyright owner. Legal action will be pursued if this is breached.

Disclaimer Notice:

Please note the information contained within this document is for educational and entertainment purposes only. Every attempt has been made to provide accurate, up-to-date and reliable, complete information. No warranties of any kind are expressed or implied. Readers acknowledge that the author is not engaging in the rendering of legal, financial, medical or professional advice.

By reading this document, the reader agrees that under no circumstances are we responsible for any losses, direct or indirect, which are incurred as a result of the use of information contained within this document, including, but not limited to, errors, omissions, or inaccuracies.

Table of Contents

Introduction	6
Chapter 1: The Mediterranean Diet Basic	**7**
What is the Mediterranean diet?	7
The history of the Mediterranean diet?	7
The Science Behind Mediterranean diet	8
Benefits of the Mediterranean diet	8
Chapter 2: The Ninja Foodi Grill Basic	**10**
The Benefits of Using an Electric Grill	10
Structural Composition of the Ninja Foodi Grill	11
How to Use the Ninja Foodi Grill?	11
Cleaning and Maintenance	13
Troubleshooting	14
Tips and Frequently Asked Questions	14

Chapter 3: Breakfast 16

Breakfast Burrito	16	Breakfast Casserole	23
Eggs & Avocado	17	Breakfast Omelette	24
Sausage Casserole	18	French Toast Sticks	25
Breakfast Potatoes	19	French Toast	26
Roasted Breakfast Potatoes	20	Ham & Cheese Casserole	27
Spicy Sausage & Mushroom Casserole	21	Breakfast Bell Peppers	28
		Crispy Garlic Potatoes	29
Hash Browns	22	Bacon	30

Chapter 4: Poultry 31

Fried Chicken	31	Buffalo Chicken Wings	39
Grilled Ranch Chicken	32	Grilled Balsamic Chicken Breast	40
Roasted Chicken	33	Chicken, Potatoes & Cabbage	41
Chicken Quesadilla	34	Barbecue Chicken Breast	42
Mustard Chicken	35	Chicken & Zucchini	43
Honey & Rosemary Chicken	36	Sugar Glazed Chicken	44
Grilled Chicken with Veggies	37	Lemon Garlic Chicken	45
Grilled Garlic Chicken	38		

Chapter 5: Meat 46

Cheeseburger	46	Steak with Asparagus	47

Grilled Herbed Steak 48
Grilled Steak & Potatoes 49
Sausage & Pepper 50
Grilled Pork Chops 51
Roast Beef with Garlic 52
Tenderloin Steak with Bacon 53
Paprika Pork Chops 54
Coffee Rib-eye 55
Rib Eye Steak with Onions & Peppers 56
Ranch Pork Chops 57
Cuban Pork Chops 58
Roast Beef & Grilled Potatoes 59
Steak Kebab 60

Chapter 6: Fish and Seafood 61
Teriyaki Salmon 61
Herbed Salmon 62
Grilled Paprika Salmon 63
Shrimp Bang Bang 64
Grilled Lemon Pepper Shrimp 65
Crumbed Flounder Fillet 66
Grilled Citrus Fish 67
Salmon with Coconut Aminos 68
Shrimp Fajitas 69
Beer-Battered Cod 70
Grilled Shrimp 71
Shrimp Boil 72
Honey Garlic Shrimp 73
Crispy Fish Fillet 74
Crispy Fish Sandwich 75

Chapter 7: Vegetables and Vegetarian 76
Roasted Mixed Veggies 76
Crispy Asparagus 77
Roasted Spicy Potatoes 78
Grilled Cauliflower Steak 79
Grilled Veggies 80
Asian Bok Choy 81
Vegetarian Bowl 82
Mediterranean Veggies 83
Mexican Corn 84
Vegetarian Pizza 85
Roasted Cauliflower 86
Garlic Brussels Sprouts 87
Honey Carrots 88
Veggie Lasagna 89
Mixed Air Fried Veggies 90

Chapter 8: Snack and Appetizer 91
Parmesan French Fries 91
Peanut Butter & Banana Snacks 92
Homemade Fries 93
Bacon Bell Peppers 94
Fried Garlic Pickles 95
Zucchini Strips with Marinara Dip . 96
Crunchy Parmesan Asparagus 97
Bacon & Sausages 98
Crispy Pickles 99
Sweet Potato Wedges 100
Fish Sticks 101
Ranch Chicken Fingers 102
Grilled Tomato Salsa 103
Greek Potatoes 104
Garlic Parmesan Fries 105

Chapter 9: Desserts 106
Strawberry & Cake Kebabs 106
Fudge Brownies 107
Cinnamon Apple Chips 108
Grilled Donuts 109

    Strawberry Pop Tarts 110
    Peanut Butter Cups 111
    Cookies 112
    Grilled Apple Pie 113
    Fried Oreos 114
    Baked Apples 115

Chapter 10: 30-Day Meal Plan 116

Conclusion 119

Introduction

Would you like to be able to quickly cook incredibly juicy Mediterranean diet, without having to spend your free time in your kitchen dealing with over-complicated recipes and sophisticated ingredients? If the answer is "YES", then you have found the right book. This Mediterranean Ninja Foodi Grill Cookbook will teach you everything you need to be able to use your Ninja Foodi Grill is best, and it will make you capable of preparing incredibly delicious Mediterranean meals that will leave your family open-mouthed even if your cooking skills are not good, or if you don't have much time to spend in your kitchen.

What are you waiting for? Forget over complex preparations and countless hours of kitchen. It's really as easy as starting to open this cookbook!

Chapter 1: The Mediterranean Diet Basic

Mediterranean diet is not just a diet plan it is one of the healthy eating lifestyles. Most of the scientific study and research conducted over the Mediterranean diet proves that the Mediterranean diet helps to reduce your excess weight, cancer cell reduction and also reduces the risk of cardiovascular diseases.

Most of the scientific study also proves that the food consumption during the Mediterranean diet like vegetables, whole grain, nuts, fish and seasonable fruits improves blood vessels functions and reduce the risk of metabolic syndrome.

What is the Mediterranean diet?

Mediterranean diet is one of the traditional diets comes from different Mediterranean countries and regions. Mediterranean diet is basically a plant-based diet that allows you high consumption of vegetables, fruits, nuts, beans, grains, fish and olive oil. Mediterranean diet is a rich fat diet, it allows near about 40 percent of calories from fat. It also allows for consuming a moderate amount of protein and low consumption of meat and dairy products.

Mediterranean diet linked with good health and a healthier heart, it helps to reduce your health issues like diabetes and heart-related disease.

The history of the Mediterranean diet?

Mediterranean diet is one of the oldest diets plans popular in worldwide. It is near about more than three thousand years old diet plan. Mediterranean is the name of the sea situated between Asia, Europe and Africa. Mediterranean diet is an eating habit of people's lives around the coast of the Mediterranean Sea like Italy, France, Spain, Greece and Morocco. There are near about 22 countries situated near the Mediterranean Sea. The large amounts of seasonable fruits are available during four seasons because of mild climate.

There are large numbers of olive trees found in Mediterranean regions. Near about 90 percent of the world, olive trees are grown in Mediterranean regions. Due to large sea coast fishing is the main occupation by most of the people in this region and fish is part of the

Mediterranean diet. Most of the scientific study conducted over Mediterranean diet proves that the diet helps to reduce the all-cause mortality. It also reduces the risk of heart-related disease and early death.

The Science Behind Mediterranean diet

Mediterranean diet is one of the high-fat diets that allow near about 40 percent of calories from fat. It is the most studied and healthiest diet worldwide.

The scientific research and study show that the peoples who follow the Mediterranean diet have lower the risk of cardiac mortality and heart disease. The study shows that the Mediterranean diet is a high-fat diet; during the diet, our body consumes a high intake of unsaturated fat and low intake of saturated fat. Unsaturated fats help to increase the HDL (Good Cholesterol) level into your body. Olive oil is one of the main fats used during the Mediterranean diet. Olive oils are full of monounsaturated fats that help to control your diabetes. It improves your insulin sensitivity and controls your diabetes. If you don't have diabetes then it helps to reduce the risk of developing diabetes.

Another study shows that the Mediterranean diet reduces the risk of stomach cancer and also reducing the risk of breast cancer in women.

Benefits of the Mediterranean diet

Mediterranean diet is one of the oldest diets in the world comes with various types of health benefits. Some of the important benefits are as follows.

- **Improves heart health**

During the Mediterranean diet, olive oil is used as a primary fat. This olive oil contains healthy fat known as monounsaturated fat helps to increase the HDL (Good Cholesterol) level and reduce the LDL (Bad Cholesterol) level. Fish is also part of the Mediterranean lifestyle, fish contains Omega-3 fatty acid which helps to improve the heart health and reduce the risk of heart failure, strokes, and sudden cardiac death.

- **Help to maintain blood sugar level**

According to the American Heart Association, the Mediterranean diet is low in sugar. It is very effective in type-2 diabetes patients and helps to maintain the blood sugar level. Mediterranean diet is rich in monounsaturated fats which help to reduce the cholesterol level and maintain your blood sugar level.

- **Increase your lifespan**

Mediterranean region's climate is clear and pollution-free climate. Due to this, you have to find fresh vegetables, seasonable fruits, beans, olives and fish in this region. All of the natural and fresh foods are full of antioxidants, which helps to reduce the inflammation in your body and slow down your aging process. It also reduces the risk of heart-related disease, inflammation, Alzheimer's and depression. The peoples live in Mediterranean regions have a longer lifespan.

- **Protects from cancer**

Mediterranean diet is one of the simple plant-based food diet. It allows high fat moderate protein and low consumption of red meat. Most of the scientific study and research show that reduction of red meat from your diet and increase the consumption of olive oil and fish into your daily diet will help to reduce the risk of several common cancers. Fish contains omega-3 fatty acids which reduce the risk of cancer.

- **Fight against depression**

The foods associated with the Mediterranean diet have anti-inflammatory properties which help to reduce the depression and help to improve your mood. One of the scientific research studies shows that the peoples who follow the Mediterranean diet have 98.6 percent of lower the risk of depression.

Chapter 2: The Ninja Foodi Grill Basic

The Ninja Foodi Grill is a tabletop multi-function appliance that can grill, air crisp, bake, roast, and even dehydrate.

It makes use of their cyclonic grilling technology that utilizes rapidly circulating hot air to cook and sea food.

The Foodi grill is an electric grill, air fryer, convection oven, oven toaster, and dehydrator all rolled into one.

The Benefits of Using an Electric Grill

Whether it is a trend or the general convenience of it, more people are appreciating smaller and more portable indoor cookers due to a number of benefits from owning one.

- Compact – Electric grills are small enough to fit most kitchen counters and tables. It is also portable enough to be easily transported or moved around.
- Smokeless – This is probably one of the best things about indoor electric grills. People who do not have any access to open areas can still enjoy grilling since it does not produce smoke like standard grillers.
- Multi-function – Most indoor cookers come with various functionalities giving you more value for your money. It can also eliminate the need to purchase other appliances and save you essential kitchen space.
- Easy to clean and operate – Indoor grills are plug and play appliances making them user-friendly to a wider demographic. The cooking components are coated with a non-stick ceramic material that can be effortlessly taken apart and cleaned using a standard dishwasher.
- Grill marks - Like traditional outdoor grills, indoor grills can also give meat and other foods those appetizing grill marks. Although, the Ninja Foodi's grill marks are curved, unlike the typical straight markings you get from regular outdoor grills.
- Browns and crisps food – Indoor grills like the Ninja Foodi use the circulating hot air to cook the food thoroughly. This creates delectable flavors through a browning process called the Maillard reaction. Similar to convection ovens and toasters, the Ninja Foodi is excellent at making food crunchy when you need it to be.
- Capable of high temperatures – A wide range of temperature settings let you cook a variety of foods from char-grilled vegetables to restaurant-level steaks. Unlike other tabletop cookers, the Ninja Grill will let you cook frozen foods without the need to defrost. It can also get as hot as 500 to 510 degrees Fahrenheit.

Structural Composition of the Ninja Foodi Grill

Although the Ninja Foodi is a countertop cooker, it does come in a hefty size. But given its multi-purpose functionality and convenience over conventional single-purpose appliances, the size can easily be excused.

The hood houses the heating element and convection fans that help sear meat and eliminate the need to flip food. The grill grates, crisper basket, and cooking pot are all coated with a non-stick ceramic finish.

All cooking components are safe to use as it is manufactured without harmful chemicals such as PTFE, PFOA, and BPA.

A grease collector at the back prevents any spillage and makes cleaning a breeze. The kebab skewers and roasting rack are all made of food-safe stainless steel as well.

The power cable is 3 meters long and is intended to keep the grill close to an outlet and prevent people from tripping over lengthy cords.

How to Use the Ninja Foodi Grill?

When you are cooking for the first time with your Foodi grill, you must first wash the detachable cooking parts with warm soapy water to remove any oil and debris. Let them air dry and place them back inside once you are ready to cook. An easy-to-follow instruction guide comes with each unit, so make sure to go over it prior to cooking.

Position your grill on a level and secure surface. Leave at least 6 inches of space around it, especially at the back where the air intake vent and air socket are located. Ensure that the splatter guard is installed whenever the grill is in use. This is a wire mesh that covers the heating element on the inside of the lid.

For grilling

- Plug your unit into an outlet and power on the grill.
- Use the grill grate over the cooking pot and choose the grill function. This has four default temperature settings of low at 400 degrees F, medium at 450 degrees F, high at 500 degrees F, and max at 510 degrees F.
- Set the time needed to cook. You may check the grilling cheat sheet that comes with your unit to guide you with the time and temperature settings. It is best to check the food regularly depending on the doneness you prefer and to avoid overcooking.
- Once the required settings are selected, press start and wait for the digital display to

show 'add food'. The unit will start to preheat similar to an oven and will show the progress through the display. This step takes about 8 minutes.

- If you need to check the food or flip it, the timer will pause and resume once the lid is closed.
- The screen will show 'Done' once the timer and cooking has completed. Power off the unit and unplug the device. Leave the hood open to let the unit cool faster.

For roasting

- Remove the grill grates and use the cooking pot that comes with the unit. You may also purchase their roasting rack for this purpose.
- Press the roast option and set the timer between 1 to 4 hours depending on the recipe requirements. The Foodi will preheat for 3 minutes regardless of the time you have set.
- Once ready, place the meat directly on the roasting pot or rack.
- Check occasionally for doneness. A meat thermometer is another useful tool to get your meats perfectly cooked.

For baking

- Remove the grates and use the cooking pot.
- Choose the bake setting and set your preferred temperature and time. Preheating will take about 3 minutes.
- Once done with preheating, you may put the ingredients directly on the cooking pot, or you may use your regular baking tray. An 8-inch baking tray can fit inside as well as similar-sized oven-safe containers.

For air frying / air crisping

- Put the crisper basket in and close the lid.
- Press the air crisp or air fry option then the start button. The default temperature is set at 390° F and will preheat at about 3 minutes. You can adjust the temperature and time by pressing the buttons beside these options.
- If you do not need to preheat, just press the air crisp button a second time and the display will show you the 'add food' message.
- Put the food inside and shake or turn every 10 minutes. Use oven mitts or tongs with silicone tips when doing this.

For dehydrating

- Place the first layer of food directly on the cooking pot.
- Add the crisper basket and add one more layer.

- Choose the dehydrate setting and set the timer between 7 to 10 hours.
- You may check the progress from time to time.

For cooking frozen foods

- Choose the medium heat, which is 450° F using the grill option. You may also use the air crisp option if you are cooking fries, vegetables, and other frozen foods.
- Set the time needed for your recipe. Add a few minutes to compensate for the thawing.
- Flip or shake after a few minutes to cook the food evenly.

Cleaning and Maintenance

Components are dishwasher-safe and are fabricated with a non-stick ceramic coating, to make clean-up and maintenance easier. Plus, the grill conveniently comes with a plastic cleaning brush with a scraper at the other end.

Cleaning tips

1. Let the grill cool down completely and ensure that it is unplugged from the power outlet before trying to clean the unit.
2. Take out the splatter guard, grill grates and cooking pot and soak in soapy water for a few hours to let the debris soften and make cleaning easier. Wash only the removable parts.
3. Gently brush off dirt and debris using the plastic brush that comes with your grill. Use the other end of the brush to dislodge food in hard to reach areas.
4. Let the parts dry thoroughly.
5. Clean the insides and exterior of the unit with a clean damp cloth.

Maintenance tips

1. Always keep your unit clean, especially before putting in a new batch for cooking. You should clean the parts and the unit after each use.
2. Never use cleaning instruments or chemicals that are too harsh and can damage the coating.
3. Keep the electrical cords away from children and any traffic in your kitchen.
4. Avoid getting the unit and electrical components wet and place it away from areas that constantly get soaked or damp.
5. Always unplug the unit when not in use.

Troubleshooting

Smoke coming out of the grill

Although the Ninja Foodi is virtually smokeless as advertised, you may see some smoke from time to time for a number of reasons.

One is the type of oil you use for cooking. Ideally, canola, grapeseed, and avocado oil should be used since they have a high smoke point. This means that they do not produce smoke or burn at high temperatures. Other oils with high smoke points include corn, almond, safflower, sesame, and sunflower oils.

Another reason is the accumulation of grease at the bottom of the pot. If you continuously cook foods that produce a lot of grease and oil, this will burn and create smoke. Empty and clean the pot before cooking the next batch.

The grill is showing 'Add Food'

This means that the unit has finished preheating and that you can now put food inside the grill.

The control panel is showing 'Shut Lid'

Try opening the lid and closing it securely until the message is gone.

Unit is unresponsive and only showing 'E' on the panel

Your unit is damaged and you need to contact customer service.

Tips and Frequently Asked Questions

Here are some useful tips you can use when cooking with the Ninja Foodi as well as some commonly asked questions to guide you if you are planning to purchase one for yourself.

Useful tips

- Brush or spray the grates with some canola, corn or avocado oil to avoid smoke.
- A light coating of oil will make your air-fried French fries taste better.
- Use the time charts as a guide, but make sure you check the food regularly since the grill gets hot and can cook quickly. You may also use a meat thermometer into your food to cook exactly the way you want.
- Use silicone or wooden utensils. Never stick metal tongs or cutleries on your grill to avoid electric shock and damaging the ceramic coating.
- If you are planning to do a lot of dehydrating and baking, it will be helpful to

- purchase their food rack and baking pan.
- If the timer was up but you need to cook the food longer, simply adjust the timer and press the start button to continue cooking.
- Although preheating is recommended to get the finest results, you can skip this step by pressing the option a second time.
- To get juicier meat, let it rest at least 5 minutes before slicing.

FAQs

1. **Is it worth the price?**

If you are getting the Foodi grill as a secondary appliance, it may seem pricey. But given the various functions you are getting with one equipment, the value for money will be apparent with continuous use.

2. **Can it heat up the kitchen as most ovens do?**

No. One great thing about portable cookers like the Ninja Foodi grill is that it does not make the kitchen uncomfortably hot making it ideal for use even during the summer time.

3. **What button should I press to pause the timer?**

Opening the lid will automatically pause the timer.

4. **Why my food is not evenly cooked when air fried?**

It is best not to overcrowd food inside the crisper basket and create an even layer to get better results. You need to flip or shake the food every few minutes to have even browning.

5. **How do I convert cooking temperatures from recipes meant for regular ovens?**

You can simply reduce the temperature required by 25 degrees Fahrenheit when using the Ninja Foodi grill. You will have to check the food regularly to make sure it will not get overcooked.

Chapter 3: Breakfast

Breakfast Burrito

Preparation Time: 15 minutes
Cooking Time: 30 minutes
Servings: 12

Ingredients:

- 1 teaspoon olive oil
- 1 lb. breakfast sausage
- 2 cups potatoes, diced
- Salt and pepper to taste
- 10 eggs, beaten
- 3 cups cheddar cheese, shredded
- 12 tortillas

Method:

1. Pour olive oil into a pan over medium heat.
2. Cook potatoes and sausage for 7 to 10 minutes, stirring frequently.
3. Spread this mixture on the bottom of the Ninja Foodi Grill pot.
4. Season with salt and pepper.
5. Pour the eggs and cheese on top.
6. Select bake setting.
7. Cook at 325 degrees F for 20 minutes.
8. Top the tortilla with the cooked mixture and roll.
9. Sprinkle cheese on the top side.
10. Add the air fryer basket to the Ninja Foodi Grill.
11. Air fry the burrito at 375 degrees F for 10 minutes.

Serving Suggestions: You can also serve this as snack.

Preparation / Cooking Tips: The burrito can be made ahead and frozen. Take it out of the freezer 30 minutes before cooking it.

Eggs & Avocado

Preparation Time: 10 minutes
Cooking Time: 15 minutes
Servings: 2

Ingredients:

- 1 avocado, sliced in half and pitted
- 2 eggs
- Salt and pepper to taste
- Cheddar cheese, shredded

Method:

1. Scoop out about a tablespoon of avocado flesh to make a hole.
2. Crack egg on top of the avocado.
3. Season with salt and pepper.
4. Sprinkle with cheese.
5. Air fry at 390 degrees F for 12 to 15 minutes.

Serving Suggestions: Serve with salsa or hot sauce.

Preparation / Cooking Tips: Scoop out more avocado flesh to create a bigger hole for the egg.

Sausage Casserole

Preparation Time: 15 minutes
Cooking Time: 20 minutes
Servings: 4

Ingredients:

- 1 lb. hash browns
- 1 lb. ground breakfast sausage, cooked
- 1 white onion, chopped
- 2 red bell peppers, chopped
- 4 eggs, beaten
- Salt and pepper to taste

Method:

1. Line the air fryer basket with foil.
2. Add hash browns at the bottom part.
3. Spread sausage, onion and bell peppers on top.
4. Air fry at 355 degrees F for 10 minutes.
5. Pour eggs on top and cook for another 10 minutes.
6. Season with salt and pepper.

Serving Suggestions: Garnish with chopped herbs.

Preparation / Cooking Tips: You can also use turkey sausage for this recipe.

Breakfast Potatoes

Preparation Time: 15 minutes
Cooking Time: 55 minutes
Servings: 4

Ingredients:

- 4 potatoes
- 4 teaspoons butter
- 2 cups cheddar cheese, shredded
- 1 1/4 cups sour cream
- 8 slices bacon, cooked crispy and chopped

Method:

1. Take out the grill gate and crisper basket.
2. Set Ninja Foodi Grill to bake.
3. Set it to 390 degrees F.
4. Preheat by selecting "start".
5. Add the potatoes inside.
6. Seal and cook for 45 minutes.
7. Let cool.
8. Make slices on top of the potatoes.
9. Create a small hole.
10. Top with butter and cheese.
11. Put the potatoes back to the pot.
12. Bake at 375 degrees F for 10 minutes.
13. Top with sour cream and bacon before serving.

Serving Suggestions: Garnish with chopped scallions.

Preparation / Cooking Tips: Preheat the Ninja Foodi Grill before putting back the potatoes back to the pot after cheese and butter have been added.

Roasted Breakfast Potatoes

Preparation Time: 15 minutes
Cooking Time: 25 minutes
Servings: 4

Ingredients:

- 3 large potatoes, diced
- 1 tablespoon olive oil
- 1 tablespoon butter
- Garlic salt and pepper to taste
- 3 sprigs thyme
- 2 sprigs rosemary

Method:

1. Add potatoes to the Ninja Foodi Grill pot.
2. Toss in olive oil and butter.
3. Season with garlic salt and pepper.
4. Top with the herb sprigs.
5. Seal the pot.
6. Set it to air fry.
7. Cook at 375 degrees F for 25 minutes.

Serving Suggestions: Garnish with chopped parsley.

Preparation / Cooking Tips: Stir the potatoes halfway through to ensure even cooking.

Spicy Sausage & Mushroom Casserole

Preparation Time: 15 minutes
Cooking Time: 15 minutes
Servings: 6

Ingredients:

- 1 tablespoon olive oil
- 3/4 cup white onion, diced
- 5 mushrooms, sliced
- 1/2 lb. spicy ground sausage
- 8 eggs, beaten scrambled
- Garlic salt to taste
- 1/4 cup cream of mushroom soup
- 3/4 cup cheddar cheese, shredded

Method:

1. In a pan over medium heat, pour the olive oil and cook onion, mushrooms and spicy ground sausage for 5 minutes.
2. Remove from heat and drain oil.
3. Pour eggs and sausage mixture into the Ninja Foodi Grill pot.
4. Season with garlic salt.
5. Spread mushroom soup on top.
6. Sprinkle with cheese.
7. Seal the pot.
8. Set to air fry and cook at 390 degrees F for 5 minutes.
9. Stir and cook for another 5 minutes.

Serving Suggestions: Sprinkle with chopped chives before serving.

Preparation / Cooking Tips: You can use Alfredo pasta sauce if you don't have cream of mushroom soup.

Hash Browns

Preparation Time: 15 minutes
Cooking Time: 20 minutes
Servings: 4

Ingredients:

- 6 potatoes, grated
- 1 onion, chopped
- 1 bell pepper, chopped
- 2 teaspoons olive oil
- Salt and pepper to taste

Method:

1. Toss the grated potatoes, onion and bell pepper separately in oil.
2. Season with salt and pepper.
3. Add potatoes to the air fryer.
4. Air fry at 400 degrees F for 10 minutes.
5. Shake and stir in onion and pepper.
6. Cook for another 10 minutes.

Serving Suggestions: Serve with side salad.

Preparation / Cooking Tips: Soak the potatoes in water for 30 minutes after grating. Dry completely with paper towels before cooking. Doing this technique results in a crispier hash brown.

Breakfast Casserole

Preparation Time: 15 minutes
Cooking Time: 15 minutes
Servings: 8

Ingredients:

- ¼ cup white onion, diced
- 1 green bell pepper, diced
- 1 lb. ground sausage, cooked
- 1/2 cup Colby Jack cheese, shredded
- 8 eggs, beaten
- Garlic salt to taste

Method:

1. Add white onion, bell pepper and ground sausage to your Ninja Foodi Grill pot.
2. Spread cheese and then the eggs on top.
3. Season with garlic salt.
4. Set to air fry and cook at 390 degrees F for 15 minutes.

Serving Suggestions: Garnish with chopped parsley.

Preparation / Cooking Tips: You can also place casserole in a small dish and put it inside the air fryer basket.

Breakfast Omelette

Preparation Time: 15 minutes
Cooking Time: 10 minutes
Servings: 6

Ingredients:

- 6 eggs
- 1 white onion, diced
- 1 red bell pepper, diced
- 6 mushrooms, chopped
- 2 slices ham, chopped and cooked
- 1 cup cheddar cheese, shredded
- Salt and pepper to taste

Method:

1. Beat eggs in a bowl.
2. Stir in the rest of the ingredients.
3. Set your Ninja Foodi Grill to air fry.
4. Pour the egg mixture into the pot.
5. Cook at 390 degrees F for 10 minutes, stirring halfway through.

Serving Suggestions: Serve with toasted garlic bread.

Preparation / Cooking Tips: You can also use turkey bacon to replace ham in this recipe.

French Toast Sticks

Preparation Time: 10 minutes
Cooking Time: 10 minutes
Servings: 12

Ingredients:

- 5 eggs
- 1 cup almond milk
- 1/4 cup sugar
- 1 teaspoon vanilla extract
- 4 tablespoons melted butter
- 4 bread slices, sliced into 12 sticks

Method:

1. Beat the eggs in a bowl.
2. Stir in milk, sugar, vanilla and butter.
3. Dip the bread sticks into the mixture.
4. Add these to the air fryer basket and place inside the Ninja Foodi Grill.
5. Air fry at 350 degrees F for 8 to 10 minutes.

Serving Suggestions: Sprinkle with cinnamon powder before serving.

Preparation / Cooking Tips: Prepare in advance and freeze for later use.

French Toast

Preparation Time: 15 minutes
Cooking Time: 10 minutes
Servings: 4

Ingredients:

- 6 eggs
- 1 cup milk
- 1 cup heavy cream
- 1 teaspoon honey
- Cooking spray
- 1 loaf French bread, sliced
- 1/2 cup butter
- 1/2 cup sugar

Method:

1. Beat the eggs in a bowl.
2. Stir in milk, cream and honey.
3. Dip the bread slices into the mixture.
4. Add to the grill basket inside the Ninja Foodi Grill.
5. Spread some butter and sprinkle sugar on top of the bread slices.
6. Seal the pot and air fry at 350 degrees F for 5 to 10 minutes.

Serving Suggestions: Serve with maple syrup.

Preparation / Cooking Tips: It's a good idea to use day-old bread for this recipe.

Ham & Cheese Casserole

Preparation Time: 15 minutes
Cooking Time: 20 minutes
Servings: 8

Ingredients:

- 1 lb. ham, chopped and cooked
- 2 cups Colby Jack cheese, shredded
- 1 white onion, chopped
- 1 red bell pepper, chopped
- 1 yellow bell pepper, chopped
- 8 eggs, beaten
- Salt and pepper to taste

Method:

1. Line the air fryer basket with foil.
2. Spread ham on the bottom of the basket.
3. Top with the cheese, onion, bell peppers and eggs.
4. Sprinkle with salt and pepper.
5. Choose air fry function.
6. Cook at 390 degrees F for 15 to 20 minutes.

Serving Suggestions: Sprinkle with grated Parmesan cheese before serving.

Preparation / Cooking Tips: You can also use cheddar cheese in place of Colby Jack cheese.

Breakfast Bell Peppers

Preparation Time: 10 minutes
Cooking Time: 15 minutes
Servings: 2

Ingredients:

- 1 large bell pepper, sliced in half
- 1 teaspoon olive oil
- 4 eggs, beaten
- Salt and pepper to taste

Method:

1. Brush the bell pepper halves with oil.
2. Pour eggs into the bell pepper.
3. Sprinkle with salt and pepper.
4. Place these in the air fryer basket.
5. Set the Ninja Foodi Grill to air fry.
6. Cook at 390 degrees F for 15 minutes.

Serving Suggestions: Sprinkle with chopped parsley before serving.

Preparation / Cooking Tips: You can also crack the eggs into the bell peppers.

Crispy Garlic Potatoes

Preparation Time: 10 minutes
Cooking Time: 20 minutes
Servings: 8

Ingredients:

- 1 1/2 lb. potatoes, diced
- 1 tablespoon avocado oil
- 1 teaspoon garlic powder
- Salt and pepper to taste

Method:

1. Toss the potatoes in oil.
2. Season with garlic powder, salt and pepper.
3. Add the air fryer basket to the Ninja Foodi Grill.
4. Select air fry setting.
5. Cook at 400 degrees F for 20 minutes, tossing halfway through.

Serving Suggestions: Sprinkle with chopped turkey bacon crisps.

Preparation / Cooking Tips: You can also season the potatoes with paprika.

Bacon

Preparation Time: 5 minutes
Cooking Time: 10 minutes
Servings: 3

Ingredients:

- 6 slices bacon
- 2 tablespoons water

Method:

1. Pour water to the bottom of the Ninja Foodi Grill pot.
2. Place the grill rack inside.
3. Put the bacon slices on the grill rack.
4. Select air fry function.
5. Cook at 350 degrees F for 5 minutes per side or until golden and crispy.

Serving Suggestions: Serve with bread and vegetables for a complete breakfast meal.

Preparation / Cooking Tips: Use turkey bacon if you want a breakfast dish that's lower in fat and cholesterol.

Chapter 4: Poultry

Fried Chicken

Preparation Time: 8 hours and 20 minutes
Cooking Time: 45 minutes
Servings: 6

Ingredients:

- 2 tablespoons onion powder
- 2 tablespoons garlic powder
- 1 tablespoon mustard powder
- 2 tablespoons chili powder
- Salt and pepper to taste
- 4 cups buttermilk
- 8 chicken thighs
- 2 cups all-purpose flour
- 3/4 cup vegetable oil
- 2 tablespoons sugar
- 3 tablespoons paprika

Method:

1. Mix the spice powders, salt and pepper in a bowl.
2. Transfer half of mixture to another bowl.
3. Pour in buttermilk to the second bowl and mix well.
4. Coat the chicken pieces with this mixture.
5. Cover and marinate in the refrigerator for 8 hours.
6. Add flour to the remaining spice blend.
7. Toss the chicken in this mixture.
8. Add to the air fryer basket.
9. Select air fryer function.
10. Cook at 360 degrees for 25 to 30 minutes.
11. Coat chicken with oil.
12. Cook for another 15 minutes.

Serving Suggestions: Serve with mustard or ketchup.

Preparation / Cooking Tips: Extend cooking time if you want your chicken crispier but be careful not to overcook.

Grilled Ranch Chicken

Preparation Time: 30 minutes
Cooking Time: 30 minutes
Servings: 6

Ingredients:

- 6 chicken thigh fillets
- 3 tablespoons ranch dressing
- Garlic salt and pepper

Method:

1. Spread both sides of chicken with ranch dressing.
2. Sprinkle with garlic salt and pepper.
3. Set your Ninja Foodi Grill to grill.
4. Preheat it to medium.
5. Add chicken to the grill grate.
6. Cook for 15 minutes per side.

Serving Suggestions: Serve with additional ranch dressing.

Preparation / Cooking Tips: Marinate the chicken for 15 to 30 minutes before cooking.

Roasted Chicken

Preparation Time: 30 minutes
Cooking Time: 1 hour and 10 minutes
Servings: 6

Ingredients:

- 1 whole chicken
- 1/2 teaspoon onion powder
- 1 teaspoon garlic powder
- 1 teaspoon paprika
- Salt and pepper to taste
- 2 drops liquid smoke
- 1 cup water
- 2 tablespoons butter
- 1/4 cup flour
- 2 cups chicken broth

Basting Butter

- 2 tablespoons butter
- Dash garlic powder

Method:

1. Season chicken with a mixture of onion powder, garlic powder, paprika, salt and pepper.
2. Add the chicken to the air frying basket.
3. Combine liquid smoke and butter.
4. Pour into the pot of your Ninja Foodi grill.
5. Seal the unit and cook at 350 degrees F for 45 minutes.
6. Drain the pot.
7. Sprinkle chicken with butter and flour.
8. Air fry at 400 degrees F for 15 minutes.
9. Baste with a mixture of the basting butter ingredients.
10. Cook for another 10 minutes.

Serving Suggestions: Serve with vegetable side dish.

Preparation / Cooking Tips: Pat the chicken dry before seasoning.

Chicken Quesadilla

Preparation Time: 20 minutes
Cooking Time: 30 minutes
Servings: 8

Ingredients:

- 4 tortillas
- Cooking spray
- 1/2 cup sour cream
- 1/2 cup salsa
- Hot sauce
- 12 oz. chicken breast fillet, chopped and grilled
- 3 jalapeño peppers, diced
- 2 cups cheddar cheese, shredded
- Chopped scallions

Method:

1. Add grill grate to the Ninja Foodi Grill.
2. Close the hood.
3. Choose grill setting.
4. Preheat for 5 minutes.
5. While waiting, spray tortillas with oil.
6. In a bowl, mix sour cream, salsa and hot sauce. Set aside.
7. Add tortilla to the grate.
8. Grill for 1 minute.
9. Repeat with the other tortillas.
10. Spread the toasted tortilla with the salsa mixture, chicken, jalapeño peppers, cheese and scallions.
11. Place a tortilla on top. Press.
12. Repeat these steps with the remaining 2 tortillas.
13. Take the grill out of the pot.
14. Choose roast setting.
15. Cook the quesadillas at 350 degrees F for 25 minutes.

Serving Suggestions: Let cool a little before slicing and serving.

Preparation / Cooking Tips: Poke holes in the tortillas to prevent ballooning.

Mustard Chicken

Preparation Time: 20 minutes
Cooking Time: 50 minutes
Servings: 4

Ingredients:

- 1/4 cup Dijon mustard
- 1/4 cup cooking oil
- Salt and pepper to taste
- 2 tablespoons honey
- 1 tablespoon dry oregano
- 2 teaspoons dry Italian seasoning
- 1 tablespoon lemon juice
- 6 chicken pieces

Method:

1. Combine all the ingredients except chicken in a bowl.
2. Mix well.
3. Toss the chicken in the mixture.
4. Add roasting rack to your Ninja Foodi Grill.
5. Choose roast function.
6. Set it to 350 degrees F.
7. Cook for 30 minutes.
8. Flip and cook for another 15 to 20 minutes.

Serving Suggestions: Serve with hot sauce.

Preparation / Cooking Tips: Use freshly squeezed lemon juice.

Honey & Rosemary Chicken

Preparation Time: 15 minutes
Cooking Time: 35 minutes
Servings: 6

Ingredients:

- 1 teaspoon paprika
- Salt to taste
- 1/2 teaspoon baking powder
- 2 lb. chicken wings
- 1/4 cup honey
- 1 tablespoon lemon juice
- 1 tablespoon garlic, minced
- 1 tablespoon rosemary, chopped

Method:

1. Choose air fry setting in your Ninja Foodi Grill.
2. Set it to 390 degrees F.
3. Set the time to 30 minutes.
4. Press start to preheat.
5. While waiting, mix the paprika, salt and baking powder in a bowl.
6. Add the wings to the crisper basket.
7. Close and cook for 15 minutes.
8. Flip and cook for another 15 minutes.
9. In a bowl, mix the remaining ingredients.
10. Coat the wings with the sauce and cook for another 5 minutes.

Serving Suggestions: Serve with the remaining sauce.

Preparation / Cooking Tips: You can also add crushed red pepper to the spice mixture.

Grilled Chicken with Veggies

Preparation Time: 20 minutes
Cooking Time: 25 minutes
Servings: 2

Ingredients:

- 2 chicken thighs and legs
- 2 tablespoons oil, divided
- Salt and pepper to taste
- 1 onion, diced
- 1/4 cup mushrooms, sliced
- 1 cup potatoes, diced
- 1 tablespoon lemon juice
- 1 tablespoon honey
- 4 sprigs fresh thyme, chopped
- 2 cloves garlic, crushed and minced

Method:

1. Add the grill grate to your Ninja Foodi Grill.
2. Put the veggie tray on top of the grill grate.
3. Close the hood.
4. Choose grill function and set it to high.
5. Press start to preheat.
6. Brush the chicken with half of oil.
7. Season with salt and pepper.
8. Toss the onion, mushrooms and potatoes in the remaining oil.
9. Sprinkle with salt and pepper.
10. Add chicken to the grill grate.
11. Add the potato mixture to the veggie tray.
12. Close the hood and cook for 10 to 15 minutes.
13. Flip chicken and toss potatoes.
14. Cook for another 10 minutes.

Serving Suggestions: Serve chicken with the veggies on the side. Garnish with herb sprigs.

Preparation / Cooking Tips: Add more cooking time if you want skin crispier.

Grilled Garlic Chicken

Preparation Time: 10 minutes
Cooking Time: 20 minutes
Servings: 8

Ingredients:

- 3 lb. chicken thigh fillets
- Garlic salt to taste

Method:

1. Add grill plate to the Ninja Foodi Grill.
2. Preheat to medium heat.
3. Sprinkle chicken with garlic salt on both sides.
4. Cook for 8 to 10 minutes.
5. Flip and cook for another 7 minutes.

Serving Suggestions: Serve with hot sauce and mustard. Serve with fries on the side.

Preparation / Cooking Tips: Add cooking time to make the skin crispier.

Buffalo Chicken Wings

Preparation Time: 15 minutes
Cooking Time: 30 minutes
Servings: 4

Ingredients:

- 2 lb. chicken wings
- 2 tablespoons oil
- 1/2 cup Buffalo sauce

Method:

1. Coat the chicken wings with oil.
2. Add these to an air fryer basket.
3. Choose air fry function.
4. Cook at 390 degrees F for 15 minutes.
5. Shake and then cook for another 15 minutes.
6. Dip in Buffalo sauce before serving.

Serving Suggestions: Serve with blue cheese dressing.

Preparation / Cooking Tips: Dry your chicken wings with paper towels before cooking.

Grilled Balsamic Chicken Breast

Preparation Time: 45 minutes
Cooking Time: 45 minutes
Servings: 4

Ingredients:

- 1/4 cup olive oil
- 2 tablespoons balsamic vinegar
- 3 teaspoon garlic, minced
- 3 tablespoons soy sauce
- 1 tablespoon Worcestershire sauce
- 1/4 cup brown sugar
- Salt and pepper to taste
- 4 chicken breast fillets

Method:

1. In a bowl, mix all ingredients except chicken.
2. Reserve 1/4 cup of the mixture for later.
3. Marinate the chicken breast in the remaining mixture for 30 minutes.
4. Add grill grate to the Ninja Foodi Grill.
5. Set it to grill and for 25 minutes.
6. Add the chicken breast and close the hood.
7. Cook for 10 minutes.
8. Flip and cook for another 5 minutes.
9. Baste with remaining sauce. Cook for 5 more minutes.
10. Serve with remaining sauce if any.

Serving Suggestions: Let chicken rest for 5 minutes before serving.

Preparation / Cooking Tips: For thick chicken breast fillets, flatten with a meat mallet.

Chicken, Potatoes & Cabbage

Preparation Time: 30 minutes
Cooking Time: 40 minutes
Servings: 8

Ingredients:

- 1 cup apple cider vinegar
- 2 lb. chicken thigh fillets
- 6 oz. barbecue sauce
- 2 lb. cabbage, sliced into wedges and steamed
- 1 lb. potatoes, roasted
- Salt and pepper to taste

Method:

1. Pour apple cider vinegar to the inner pot.
2. Add grill grate to the Ninja Foodi Grill.
3. Place the chicken on top of the grill.
4. Sprinkle both sides with salt and pepper.
5. Grill the chicken for 15 to 20 minutes per side at 350 degrees F.
6. Baste the chicken with the barbecue sauce.
7. Serve chicken with potatoes and cabbage.

Serving Suggestions: Serve with hot sauce and mustard.

Preparation / Cooking Tips: You can also brush veggies with barbecue sauce if you like.

Barbecue Chicken Breast

Preparation Time: 15 minutes
Cooking Time: 50 minutes
Servings: 4

Ingredients:

- 4 chicken breast fillets
- 2 tablespoons vegetable oil
- Salt and pepper to taste
- 1 cup barbecue sauce

Method:

1. Add grill grate to the Ninja Foodi Grill.
2. Close the hood.
3. Choose grill setting.
4. Preheat to medium for 25 minutes.
5. Press start.
6. Brush chicken breast with oil.
7. Sprinkle both sides with salt and pepper.
8. Add chicken and cook for 10 minutes.
9. Flip and cook for another 10 minutes.
10. Brush chicken with barbecue sauce.
11. Cook for 5 minutes.
12. Brush the other side and cook for another 5 minutes.

Serving Suggestions: Serve with mashed potato and gravy.

Preparation / Cooking Tips: You can also use homemade barbecue sauce simply by mixing ketchup, sugar, minced garlic, lemon juice and soy sauce.

Chicken & Zucchini

Preparation Time: 30 minutes
Cooking Time: 20 minutes
Servings: 6

Ingredients:

- 1/4 cup olive oil
- 1 tablespoon lemon juice
- 2 tablespoons red wine vinegar
- 1 teaspoon oregano
- 1 tablespoon garlic, chopped
- 2 chicken breast fillet, sliced into cubes
- 1 zucchini, sliced
- 1 red onion, sliced
- 1 cup cherry tomatoes, sliced
- Salt and pepper to taste

Method:

1. In a bowl, mix the olive oil, lemon juice, vinegar, oregano and garlic.
2. Pour half of mixture into another bowl.
3. Toss chicken in half of the mixture.
4. Cover and marinate for 15 minutes.
5. Toss the veggies in the remaining mixture.
6. Season both chicken and veggies with salt and pepper.
7. Add chicken to the air fryer basket.
8. Spread veggies on top.
9. Select air fry function.
10. Seal and cook at 380 degrees F for 15 to 20 minutes.

Serving Suggestions: Garnish with lemon wedges.

Preparation / Cooking Tips: If you want to marinate longer, cover and refrigerate for 1 hour.

Sugar Glazed Chicken

Preparation Time: 15 minutes
Cooking Time: 45 minutes
Servings: 8

Ingredients:

- 1 tablespoon olive oil
- 1/2 tablespoon apple cider vinegar
- 3 teaspoon garlic, minced
- 1 tablespoon honey
- 1/4 cup light brown sugar
- 1/3 cup soy sauce
- 8 chicken thigh fillets

Method:

1. Combine all the ingredients except chicken.
2. Reserve 1/4 cup of this mixture for later.
3. Marinate the chicken with the remaining mixture for 30 minutes.
4. Add grill grate to your Ninja Foodi Grill.
5. Select grill button.
6. Set it to 25 minutes.
7. Add chicken to the grill.
8. Close the hood.
9. Cook for 10 minutes.
10. Flip and cook for 5 minutes.
11. Brush with the remaining mixture.
12. Cook for another 5 minutes.

Serving Suggestions: Let chicken rest for 10 minutes before slicing and serving.

Preparation / Cooking Tips: You can also add a dash of hot sauce.

Lemon Garlic Chicken

Preparation Time: 15 minutes
Cooking Time: 40 minutes
Servings: 4

Ingredients:

- 4 chicken breast fillets
- 1 tablespoon lemon juice
- 1 tablespoon melted butter
- 1 teaspoon garlic powder
- Salt and pepper to taste

Method:

1. Mix lemon juice and melted butter in a bowl.
2. Brush both sides of chicken with this mixture.
3. Season with garlic powder, salt and pepper.
4. Insert grill grate to your Ninja Foodi Grill.
5. Place chicken on top of the grill.
6. Close the hood.
7. Grill at 350 degrees F for 15 to 20 minutes per side.

Serving Suggestions: Garnish with lemon slices.

Preparation / Cooking Tips: You can also use margarine in place of butter.

Chapter 5: Meat

Cheeseburger

Preparation Time: 20 minutes
Cooking Time: 10 minutes
Servings: 4

Ingredients:

- 1 1/2 lb. ground beef
- 1 onion, minced
- 1 red bell pepper, chopped
- 1 tablespoon breadcrumbs
- 1 egg, beaten
- Salt and pepper to taste
- 4 cheese slices
- 4 burger buns

Method:

1. Insert grill grate to your Ninja Foodi Grill.
2. Choose grill setting.
3. Set it to high. Set time to 10 minutes.
4. Preheat your unit.
5. In a bowl, mix ground beef, onion, bell pepper, breadcrumbs and egg.
6. Form patties from the mixture.
7. Season patties with salt and pepper.
8. Add patties to the grill.
9. Cook for 8 to 10 minutes.
10. Add cheese on top of the beef and cook for another 1 minute.
11. Serve patties and cheese on burger buns.

Serving Suggestions: Serve with desired condiments.

Preparation / Cooking Tips: Use lean ground beef.

Steak with Asparagus

Preparation Time: 20 minutes
Cooking Time: 20 minutes
Servings: 4

Ingredients:

- 2 strip steaks
- 2 tablespoons vegetable oil, divided
- Pinch steak seasoning
- Salt and pepper to taste
- 2 cups asparagus, trimmed and sliced

Method:

1. Coat strip steaks with half of oil.
2. Season with steak seasoning, salt and pepper.
3. Toss asparagus with oil, salt and pepper.
4. Add grill grate to the Ninja Foodi Grill. Seal the hood.
5. Select grill function and preheat it to high for 10 minutes.
6. Add steaks to the grill.
7. Cook for 5 minutes.
8. Flip and cook for 5 more minutes.
9. Add asparagus to the veggie tray.
10. Place veggie tray on top of the grill grate.
11. Cook for 10 minutes.
12. Serve steak with asparagus.

Serving Suggestions: Serve with salad or brown rice.

Preparation / Cooking Tips: Press steaks onto the grill to give it grill marks.

Grilled Herbed Steak

Preparation Time: 15 minutes
Cooking Time: 10 minutes
Servings: 4

Ingredients:

- 4 steaks
- Garlic salt to taste
- 4 sprigs rosemary, chopped
- 1 teaspoon dried tarragon
- 1 teaspoon dried basil

Method:

1. Add grill grate to the Ninja Foodi Grill.
2. Close the hood and choose grill setting.
3. Set it to 15 minutes.
4. Set it to high.
5. Press start to preheat.
6. Rub both sides of steak with garlic salt.
7. Sprinkle with herbs.
8. Add steaks to the grill grate.
9. Cook for 5 minutes per side.

Serving Suggestions: Garnish with fresh rosemary sprig.

Preparation / Cooking Tips: Marinate steak in herbs for 15 minutes before cooking.

Grilled Steak & Potatoes

Preparation Time: 20 minutes
Cooking Time: 50 minutes
Servings: 4

Ingredients:

- 4 potatoes
- 3 sirloin steaks
- 1/4 cup avocado oil
- 2 tablespoons steak seasoning
- Salt to taste

Method:

1. Poke potatoes with fork.
2. Coat potatoes with half of avocado oil.
3. Season with salt.
4. Add to the air fryer basket.
5. Choose air fry function in your Ninja Foodi Grill.
6. Seal the hood and cook at 400 degrees F for 35 minutes.
7. Flip and cook for another 10 minutes.
8. Transfer to a plate.
9. Add grill grate to the Ninja Foodi Grill.
10. Add steaks to the grill grate.
11. Set it to high.
12. Cook for 7 minutes per side.
13. Serve steaks with potatoes.

Serving Suggestions: Serve with steak sauce and hot sauce.

Preparation / Cooking Tips: Press steaks onto the grill to give it grill marks.

Sausage & Pepper

Preparation Time: 30 minutes
Cooking Time: 20 minutes
Servings: 6

Ingredients:

- 1 white onion, sliced into rings
- 2 bell peppers, sliced
- 2 tablespoons vegetable oil
- Salt and pepper to taste
- 6 Italian sausages

Method:

1. Add grill grate to your Ninja Foodi Grill.
2. Close the hood.
3. Choose grill setting.
4. Set it to low. Set it to 25 minutes. Press start to preheat.
5. Toss onions and bell peppers in oil.
6. Season with salt and pepper.
7. Add veggies to the grill grate.
8. Cook for 10 minutes.
9. Transfer veggies to a bowl.
10. Grill sausages for 5 minutes per side.
11. Top sausages with veggies.

Serving Suggestions: Serve as is or in hot dog buns.

Preparation / Cooking Tips: You can also use Bratwurst for this recipe.

Grilled Pork Chops

Preparation Time: 10 minutes
Cooking Time: 15 minutes
Servings: 4

Ingredients:

- 4 pork chops
- Salt and pepper to taste
- Barbecue sauce

Method:

1. Add grill grate to your Ninja Foodi Grill.
2. Set it to grill. Close the hood.
3. Preheat to high for 15 minutes.
4. Season pork chops with salt and pepper.
5. Add to the grill grates.
6. Grill for 8 minutes.
7. Flip and cook for another 7 minutes, brushing both sides with barbecue sauce.

Serving Suggestions: Let rest for 5 minutes before slicing and serving.

Preparation / Cooking Tips: You can also make your own barbecue sauce by mixing soy sauce, sugar or honey, lemon juice and ketchup.

Roast Beef with Garlic

Preparation Time: 15 minutes
Cooking Time: 1 hour and 20 minutes
Servings: 4

Ingredients:

- 2 lb. beef roast, sliced
- 2 tablespoons vegetable oil
- Salt and pepper to taste
- 6 cloves garlic

Method:

1. Coat beef roast with oil.
2. Season with salt and pepper.
3. Place inside the Ninja Foodi Grill pot.
4. Sprinkle garlic on top.
5. Choose bake setting.
6. Set it to 400 degrees F and cook for 30 minutes.
7. Reduce temperature to 375 degrees F and cook for another 40 minutes.

Serving Suggestions: Serve with mashed potato and gravy.

Preparation / Cooking Tips: If refrigerated, let beef come to room temperature 2 hours before cooking.

Tenderloin Steak with Bacon

Preparation Time: 15 minutes
Cooking Time: 20 minutes
Servings: 4

Ingredients:

- 8 bacon strips
- 4 tenderloin steaks
- 2 tablespoons vegetable oil
- Salt and pepper to taste

Method:

1. Wrap the tenderloin steak with bacon strips.
2. Coat the steaks with oil.
3. Sprinkle with salt and pepper.
4. Insert grill grate in the Ninja Foodi Grill.
5. Choose grill setting.
6. Set it to high for 12 minutes.
7. Press start to preheat.
8. Add the steaks on the grill.
9. Cook for 6 to 8 minutes per side.

Serving Suggestions: Serve with side vegetable salad.

Preparation / Cooking Tips: You can use a toothpick to secure the bacon around the steaks.

Paprika Pork Chops

Preparation Time: 15 minutes
Cooking Time: 15 minutes
Servings: 2

Ingredients:

- 2 pork chops
- 1 teaspoon olive oil
- 1 teaspoon smoked paprika
- 1 teaspoon garlic powder
- Salt and pepper to taste

Method:

1. Brush pork chops with oil.
2. Sprinkle with paprika, garlic powder, salt and pepper.
3. Set your Ninja Foodi Grill to air fry.
4. Add pork chops to the air fryer basket.
5. Cook at 360 degrees F for 15 minutes.
6. Flip and cook for another 15 minutes.
7. Let sit for 3 to 5 minutes before serving.

Serving Suggestions: Serve with cucumber and tomato slices.

Preparation / Cooking Tips: Marinate for 15 minutes before air frying.

Coffee Rib-eye

Preparation Time: 20 minutes
Cooking Time: 30 minutes
Servings: 4

Ingredients:

- 4 rib eye steaks
- 1 tablespoon vegetable oil
- 2 tablespoons coffee
- 1 teaspoon onion powder
- 1 teaspoon garlic powder
- 2 tablespoons ground chipotle pepper
- 1/2 teaspoon ground ginger
- 1/2 teaspoon mustard powder
- Salt and pepper to taste

Method:

1. Brush both sides of steak with oil.
2. In a bowl, mix the remaining ingredients.
3. Sprinkle steak with spice mixture.
4. Add grill grate to your Ninja Foodi Grill.
5. Seal the hood and choose grill setting.
6. Set it to high. Start to preheat.
7. Add grill to the grate.
8. Once the temperate reaches 11o degrees F, flip the beef.
9. Wait until the pot beeps.
10. Let it rest for 10 minutes before slicing and serving.

Serving Suggestions: Serve with steamed veggies.

Preparation / Cooking Tips: Press steaks to give it grill marks.

Rib Eye Steak with Onions & Peppers

Preparation Time: 20 minutes
Cooking Time: 20 minutes
Servings: 2

Ingredients:

- 1/2 teaspoon cumin
- 1/2 teaspoon onion powder
- 1/2 teaspoon garlic powder
- 1 teaspoon smoked paprika
- Salt and pepper to taste
- 2 rib eye steaks
- 1 tablespoon vegetable oil
- 1 white onion, sliced into rings
- 1 red bell pepper, sliced
- 1/4 cup fajita sauce

Method:

1. Combine cumin, onion powder, garlic powder, paprika, salt and pepper to taste.
2. Add grill grate to your Ninja Foodi Grill.
3. Place the veggie tray on the grill grate. Seal the hood.
4. Choose grill setting.
5. Preheat it to medium for 20 minutes.
6. Coat steaks with half of oil.
7. Sprinkle with half of spice blend.
8. Toss the onions and bell pepper with remaining oil and spice blend.
9. Add steaks on the grill grate.
10. Cook for 10 minutes.
11. Brush both sides with fajita sauce.
12. Cook for another 10 minutes.
13. Add veggies to the veggie tray.
14. Cook with the steak for 10 minutes.

Serving Suggestions: Serve with fresh green salad or pasta.

Preparation / Cooking Tips: Increase cooking time if you want your steaks well-done.

Ranch Pork Chops

Preparation Time: 20 minutes
Cooking Time: 20 minutes
Servings: 4

Ingredients:

- 1 teaspoon garlic powder
- 1 cup breadcrumbs
- 1 tablespoon Parmesan cheese, grated
- Salt and pepper to taste
- 1 tablespoon buttermilk
- 1/2 cup ranch dressing
- 4 pork chops

Method:

1. Mix garlic powder, breadcrumbs, Parmesan cheese, salt and pepper in a bowl.
2. Combine buttermilk and ranch dressing in another wall.
3. Dip the pork chops in the buttermilk mixture.
4. Dredge with the breadcrumb mixture.
5. Set the Ninja Foodi Grill to air fry.
6. Cook at 330 degrees F for 10 minutes per side.

Serving Suggestions: Serve with vegetable salad.

Preparation / Cooking Tips: You can also use other types of milk for this recipe.

Cuban Pork Chops

Preparation Time: 8 hours and 20 minutes
Cooking Time: 30 minutes
Servings: 4

Ingredients:

- 4 pork chops
- 1/2 cup olive oil
- 8 cloves garlic, minced
- 1 cup orange juice
- 1/2 cup lime juice
- 1 teaspoon orange zest
- 1 teaspoon lime zest
- 1/4 cup mint leaves, chopped
- 2 teaspoons dried oregano
- 2 teaspoons ground cumin
- 1 cup cilantro, chopped

Method:

1. Place pork chops in a shallow plate.
2. In another bowl, mix the remaining ingredients.
3. Take ¼ cup of the mixture and set aside.
4. Add the remaining mixture to the pork chops.
5. Cover and marinate in the refrigerator for 8 hours.
6. Add grill grate to the Ninja Foodi Grill. Seal the hood.
7. Choose grill setting.
8. Set it to high.
9. Set the time to 15 minutes.
10. Close the hood and cook for 15 minutes, flipping once.

Serving Suggestions: Let rest for 5 minutes before slicing and serving.

Preparation / Cooking Tips: You can also marinate only for 1 hour if you want shorter preparation time.

Roast Beef & Grilled Potatoes

Preparation Time: 15 minutes
Cooking Time: 45 minutes
Servings: 6

Ingredients:

- 2 1/2 teaspoons onion powder
- 2 1/2 teaspoons garlic powder
- Salt and pepper to taste
- 3 lb. top round roast
- 4 cups potatoes, grilled

Method:

1. Combine onion powder, garlic powder, salt and pepper in a bowl.
2. Rub top round roast with dry rub.
3. Set the Ninja Foodi Grill to broil.
4. Preheat it to high for 10 minutes.
5. Add the roast beef and cook for 25 minutes.
6. Turn and cook for another 20 minutes.
7. Serve with grilled potatoes.

Serving Suggestions: Slice against the grain and serve.

Preparation / Cooking Tips: Let the roast come to room temperature for 1 hour before seasoning.

Steak Kebab

Preparation Time: 30 minutes
Cooking Time: 15 minutes
Servings: 4

Ingredients:

- 2 strip steaks, sliced into cubes
- 1 white onion, sliced into wedges
- 1 bell pepper, sliced
- 8 button mushrooms
- Dash steak seasoning
- Salt and pepper to taste

Method:

1. Add grill grate to the Ninja Foodi Grill.
2. Close the hood and press grill setting.
3. Set it to high. Set it to 12 minutes. Press start to preheat.
4. While waiting, thread steak and veggies onto skewers.
5. Season with steak seasoning, salt and pepper.
6. Place on top of the grill grate.
7. Cook for 8 minutes.
8. Flip and cook for another 6 to 7 minutes.

Serving Suggestions: Serve with brown rice.

Preparation / Cooking Tips: Brush with barbecue basting sauce halfway through grilling.

Chapter 6: Fish and Seafood

Teriyaki Salmon

Preparation Time: 10 minutes
Cooking Time: 10 minutes
Servings: 4

Ingredients:

- 4 salmon fillets
- 1 cup teriyaki sauce

Method:

1. Coat fish fillet with teriyaki sauce.
2. Cover and refrigerate for 12 hours.
3. Add grill grate to the Ninja Foodi Grill.
4. Select grill setting. Set it to high.
5. Set the time to 10 minutes.
6. Press start to preheat.
7. Put the fish fillets on the grill.
8. Cook for 6 minutes.
9. Flip and cook for 2 minutes.

Serving Suggestions: Garnish with white sesame seeds or chopped scallions.

Preparation / Cooking Tips: You can also use barbecue sauce for this recipe.

Herbed Salmon

Preparation Time: 15 minutes
Cooking Time: 10 minutes
Servings: 2

Ingredients:

- 2 salmon fillets
- 2 tablespoons olive oil
- 1 teaspoon Herbes de Provence
- 1/4 teaspoon smoked paprika
- Salt and pepper to taste
- 1 tablespoon butter
- 1/2 teaspoon lemon juice

Method:

1. Coat the salmon with olive oil.
2. Sprinkle with herbs, paprika, salt and pepper.
3. Insert grill grate to the Ninja Foodi Grill.
4. Set it to high. Set it to 10 minutes.
5. Press start to preheat.
6. Add fish to the grill.
7. Grill for 3 to 5 minutes per side.
8. Top the fish with the butter and drizzle with lemon juice before serving.

Serving Suggestions: Garnish with lemon slices and chopped parsley.

Preparation / Cooking Tips: Press the fish onto the grill if you want it to have grill marks.

Grilled Paprika Salmon

Preparation Time: 10 minutes
Cooking Time: 10 minutes
Servings: 2

Ingredients:

- 2 salmon fillets
- Pinch paprika
- Salt and pepper to taste

Method:

1. Insert grill grate to the Ninja Foodi Grill.
2. Choose grill function.
3. Set it to high and preheat for 10 minutes.
4. Season salmon with paprika, salt and pepper.
5. Add salmon to the grill.
6. Cook for 5 minutes per side.

Serving Suggestions: Serve with pasta salad.

Preparation / Cooking Tips: You can also use white fish fillet for this recipe.

Shrimp Bang Bang

Preparation Time: 15 minutes
Cooking Time: 30 minutes
Servings: 4

Ingredients:

- 1/2 cup all-purpose flour
- 2 eggs, beaten
- 2 tablespoons olive oil
- 1 cup breadcrumbs
- Salt and pepper to taste
- 1 teaspoon garlic powder
- 1 lb. shrimp, peeled and deveined
- 1/2 cup mayonnaise
- 1/2 cup sweet chili sauce
- 1 tablespoon lime juice
- 1 tablespoon hot pepper sauce
- Salt to taste
- 2 teaspoons honey

Method:

1. Add flour to a bowl.
2. Put the eggs in a second bowl.
3. Mix the breadcrumbs, salt, pepper and garlic powder in the third bowl.
4. Coat shrimp with flour and then with egg.
5. Dredge with breadcrumb blend.
6. Set Ninja Foodi Grill to air fry.
7. Cook at 400 degrees F for 15 minutes.
8. Shake and cook for another 15 minutes.
9. Combine the rest of the ingredients in a bowl.
10. Dip the shrimp in this mixture and serve.

Serving Suggestions: Serve with more hot sauce if desired.

Preparation / Cooking Tips: Use light mayonnaise for this recipe.

Grilled Lemon Pepper Shrimp

Preparation Time: 15 minutes
Cooking Time: 10 minutes
Servings: 4

Ingredients:

- 1 lb. shrimp, peeled and deveined
- Cooking spray
- Pinch lemon pepper seasoning

Method:

1. Spray the shrimp with oil.
2. Sprinkle with lemon pepper seasoning.
3. Set Ninja Foodi Grill to air fry.
4. Cook at 350 degrees F for 3 to 5 minutes per side.

Serving Suggestions: Serve with mango salsa.

Preparation / Cooking Tips: Marinate shrimp for 15 minutes before cooking.

Crumbed Flounder Fillet

Preparation Time: 10 minutes
Cooking Time: 12 minutes
Servings: 4

Ingredients:

- ¼ cup vegetable oil
- 1 cup breadcrumbs
- 4 flounder fillets
- 1 egg, beaten

Method:

1. Set Ninja Foodi Grill to air fry.
2. Preheat to 350 degrees F.
3. Combine oil and breadcrumbs in a bowl.
4. Mix until crumbly.
5. Coat the fish with egg and dredge with the breadcrumb mixture.
6. Add fish fillets to the air fryer basket.
7. Cook for 12 minutes.

Serving Suggestions: Garnish with lemon wedges.

Preparation / Cooking Tips: You can also use olive oil in place of vegetable oil.

Grilled Citrus Fish

Preparation Time: 20 minutes
Cooking Time: 15 minutes
Servings: 2

Ingredients:

- 2 tablespoons oil
- 2 tablespoons honey
- 1 tablespoon orange juice
- 1 tablespoon lemon juice
- 1 teaspoon orange zest
- 1 teaspoon lemon zest
- 1 teaspoon garlic, minced
- 1 teaspoon ginger, minced
- 1 tablespoon parsley, minced
- Salt and pepper to taste
- 2 white fish fillets

Method:

1. Add grill grate to the Ninja Foodi Grill.
2. Choose grill function.
3. Set it to high.
4. Set the time to 15 minutes and press start.
5. Mix all the ingredients except fish fillets.
6. Spread half of the mixture on both sides of the fish.
7. Add fish fillets to the grill grate.
8. Close the hood and grill for 15 minutes, brushing with the remaining mixture.

Serving Suggestions: Serve with steamed veggies. Garnish with lemon and orange slices.

Preparation / Cooking Tips: You can use halibut or any white fish fillet for this recipe.

Salmon with Coconut Aminos

Preparation Time: 45 minutes
Cooking Time: 15 minutes
Servings: 4

Ingredients:

- 1/2 teaspoon ginger powder
- 1/2 teaspoon garlic powder
- 1 tablespoon honey
- 4 tablespoons coconut aminos
- Salt and pepper to taste
- 3 salmon fillets

Method:

1. In a bowl, mix ginger powder, garlic powder, honey, coconut aminos, salt and pepper in a bowl.
2. Coat the salmon fillets with this mixture.
3. Marinate for 30 minutes, covered in the refrigerator.
4. Add fish to the air fryer basket.
5. Set your Ninja Foodi Grill to air fry.
6. Cook at 390 degrees F for 10 to 15 minutes.

Serving Suggestions: Garnish with lemon slices.

Preparation / Cooking Tips: Do not overcrowd the air fryer basket to ensure even cooking. Cook in batches if necessary.

Shrimp Fajitas

Preparation Time: 20 minutes
Cooking Time: 20 minutes
Servings: 12

Ingredients:

- 1 lb. shrimp, peeled and deveined
- 1 onion, diced
- 1 red bell pepper, chopped
- 1 green bell pepper, chopped
- 2 tablespoons taco seasoning
- Cooking spray
- Tortillas

Method:

1. Spray air fryer basket with oil.
2. Mix shrimp, onion and bell peppers in a bowl.
3. Spray with oil and season with taco seasoning.
4. Set your Ninja Foodi Grill to air fry.
5. Add shrimp mixture to the air fryer basket.
6. Air fry at 390 degrees F for 10 to 12 minutes.
7. Shake and cook for another 10 minutes.
8. Spread on top of tortillas.

Serving Suggestions: Serve with hot sauce.

Preparation / Cooking Tips: If you're going to use frozen shrimp, add 3 to 5 more minutes of cooking time.

Beer-Battered Cod

Preparation Time: 15 minutes
Cooking Time: 15 minutes
Servings: 4

Ingredients:

- 1 cup all-purpose flour
- ½ teaspoon baking soda
- 2 tablespoons cornstarch
- 1 egg, beaten
- 6 oz. beer
- 4 cod fillets
- ½ teaspoon paprika
- Pinch cayenne pepper
- Salt and pepper to taste
- Vegetable oil

Method:

1. Mix flour, baking soda, cornstarch, egg and beer in a bowl.
2. Sprinkle cod fillets with paprika, cayenne, salt and pepper.
3. Dip in the flour mixture.
4. Drizzle with oil.
5. Add to the air fryer basket.
6. Choose air fry setting in your Ninja Foodi Grill.
7. Cook at 390 degrees F for 12 to 15 minutes.

Serving Suggestions: Serve with coleslaw.

Preparation / Cooking Tips: Refrigerate flour mixture for 20 minutes before using.

Grilled Shrimp

Preparation Time: 20 minutes
Cooking Time: 10 minutes
Servings: 8

Ingredients:

- 2 lb. shrimp, deveined
- 2 tablespoons olive oil
- 1 tablespoon Old Bay Seasoning
- Garlic salt to taste

Method:

1. Preheat your grill to medium.
2. Brush shrimp with olive oil.
3. Season with Old Bay seasoning and garlic salt.
4. Cook for 3 to 5 minutes per side.

Serving Suggestions: Serve with grilled corn.

Preparation / Cooking Tips: Add cayenne pepper if you want your shrimp spicier.

Shrimp Boil

Preparation Time: 10 minutes
Cooking Time: 15 minutes
Servings: 6

Ingredients:

- 12 oz. shrimp, peeled and deveined
- 14 oz. smoked sausage, sliced
- 4 corn on cobs, sliced into 4
- 3 cups potatoes, sliced in half and boiled
- 1/8 cup Old Bay seasoning
- 1/4 cup white onion, diced
- Cooking spray

Method:

1. Mix all the ingredients in the inner pot of the Ninja Foodi Grill.
2. Spray mixture with oil.
3. Set the unit to air fry.
4. Air fry at 390 degrees F for 5 to 7 minutes.
5. Stir and cook for another 6 minutes.

Serving Suggestions: Sprinkle with dried herbs before serving.

Preparation / Cooking Tips: Check the dish halfway through cooking to see if it's cooking evenly.

Honey Garlic Shrimp

Preparation Time: 15 minutes
Cooking Time: 30 minutes
Servings: 6

Ingredients:

- 1/2 cup tamari
- 1/2 cup honey
- 1 clove garlic, crushed
- 1 teaspoon fresh ginger
- 2 tablespoons ketchup
- 2 tablespoons cornstarch
- 16 oz. shrimp, peeled and deveined
- 16 oz. frozen vegetables

Method:

1. Add tamari, honey, garlic, ginger and ketchup in a pan over medium heat.
2. Simmer for 10 minutes.
3. Stir in cornstarch and simmer for 5 minutes.
4. Dip shrimp in the sauce.
5. Add shrimp to the air fryer basket.
6. Set your Ninja Foodi Grill to air fry.
7. Air fry at 355 degrees F for 10 to 12 minutes.

Serving Suggestions: Serve with hot brown rice.

Preparation / Cooking Tips: You can also use pre-peeled shrimp to save time.

Crispy Fish Fillet

Preparation Time: 15 minutes
Cooking Time: 5 minutes
Servings: 6

Ingredients:

- 6 fish fillets
- 1 egg, beaten
- 2 tablespoons Old Bay seasoning
- 1 cup breadcrumbs
- Cooking spray

Method:

1. Set the Ninja Foodi Grill to air fry.
2. Dip the fish fillets in egg.
3. Mix the seasoning and breadcrumbs.
4. Add the fish to the air fryer basket.
5. Cook at 400 degrees F for 5 minutes.

Serving Suggestions: Serve with stir fried vegetables and with sweet chili sauce.

Preparation / Cooking Tips: Dry the fish fillets with paper towel before seasoning and dredging with breadcrumbs.

Crispy Fish Sandwich

Preparation Time: 15 minutes
Cooking Time: 12 minutes
Servings: 2

Ingredients:

Tartar Sauce

- 1/4 cup mayonnaise
- 1 teaspoon pickle juice
- 2 tablespoons dill pickles, chopped

Fish Sandwiches

- 2 white fish fillets
- 2 teaspoons Old Bay Seasoning
- 2 tablespoons flour
- 1 egg, beaten
- 1/2 cup breadcrumbs
- 2 slices low-fat cheese slices
- 2 burger buns

Method:

1. Mix mayo, pickle juice and dill pickles in a bowl.
2. Cover and place inside the refrigerator.
3. Add seasoning and flour in a dish.
4. Beat egg in a bowl.
5. Put breadcrumbs in the third bowl.
6. Coat fish fillets with flour mixture.
7. Dip in egg and then dredge with breadcrumbs.
8. Add fish fillets to the air fryer basket.
9. Set Ninja Foodi Grill to air fry.
10. Cook at 350 degrees F for 10 to 12 minutes.
11. Add crispy fish to burger buns.
12. Top with tartar sauce and cheese.

Serving Suggestions: Serve with cucumber and tomato salad.

Preparation / Cooking Tips: Use low-fat or fat-free mayonnaise.

Chapter 7: Vegetables and Vegetarian

Roasted Mixed Veggies

Preparation Time: 15 minutes
Cooking Time: 15 minutes
Servings: 4

Ingredients:

- 1 zucchini, sliced
- 8 oz. mushrooms, sliced
- 2 tablespoons olive oil
- 1 tablespoon garlic, minced
- 1 teaspoon onion powder
- 1 teaspoon garlic powder
- Salt and pepper to taste

Method:

1. Choose air fry setting in your Ninja Foodi Grill.
2. Insert air fryer basket.
3. Preheat it to 390 degrees F.
4. Toss zucchini and mushrooms in oil.
5. Sprinkle with garlic.
6. Season with onion powder, garlic powder, salt and pepper.
7. Place in the basket.
8. Cook for 10 minutes.
9. Stir and cook for another 5 minutes.

Serving Suggestions: Serve as side dish to a main course.

Preparation / Cooking Tips: Do not overcrowd the basket with veggies.

Crispy Asparagus

Preparation Time: 10 minutes
Cooking Time: 10 minutes
Servings: 4

Ingredients:

- 1 lb. asparagus, trimmed
- 2 teaspoons olive oil
- Salt and pepper to taste

Method:

1. Coat asparagus with oil.
2. Sprinkle with salt and pepper.
3. Choose air fry setting in your Ninja Foodi Grill.
4. Set it to 390 degrees F.
5. Cook asparagus in the air fryer basket for 7 to 10 minutes, shaking halfway through.

Serving Suggestions: Sprinkle with Parmesan cheese on top before serving.

Preparation / Cooking Tips: Dry asparagus before seasoning.

Roasted Spicy Potatoes

Preparation Time: 15 minutes
Cooking Time: 25 minutes
Servings: 4

Ingredients:

- 1 lb. baby potatoes, sliced into wedges
- 2 tablespoons olive oil
- Salt to taste
- 1 tablespoon garlic powder
- 1 tablespoon paprika
- 1/2 cup mayonnaise
- 2 tablespoons white wine vinegar
- 2 tablespoons tomato paste
- 1 teaspoon chili powder

Method:

1. Toss potatoes in oil.
2. Sprinkle with salt, garlic powder and paprika.
3. Add crisper plate to the air fryer basket.
4. Add basket to the Ninja Foodi Grill.
5. Set it to air fry.
6. Set it to 360 degrees F for 30 minutes.
7. Press start to preheat.
8. Put the potatoes on the crisper plate after 3 minutes.
9. Cook for 25 minutes.
10. While waiting, mix the remaining ingredients.
11. Toss potatoes in spicy mayo mixture and serve.

Serving Suggestions: Sprinkle with chopped parsley before serving.

Preparation / Cooking Tips: Poke potatoes with a fork before roasting.

Grilled Cauliflower Steak

Preparation Time: 30 minutes
Cooking Time: 25 minutes
Servings: 2

Ingredients:

- 2 cauliflower steaks
- 1/4 cup vegetable oil, divided
- Salt and pepper to taste
- 1 onion, chopped
- 3 cloves garlic, minced
- 1/2 cup roasted red bell peppers, chopped
- 1/4 cup Kalamata olives, chopped
- 1 tablespoon fresh parsley, chopped
- 1 tablespoon fresh oregano, chopped
- 1/2 lb. feta cheese, crumbled
- 1 tablespoon lemon juice
- 1/4 cup walnuts, chopped

Method:

1. Add grill grate to your Ninja Foodi Grill.
2. Choose grill setting.
3. Set it to max for 17 minutes.
4. Press start to preheat.
5. Brush both sides of cauliflower steaks with oil.
6. Season with salt and pepper.
7. Grill for 10 minutes per side.
8. Mix the remaining ingredients in a bowl.
9. Spread mixture on top of the steaks and cook for another 2 minutes.

Serving Suggestions: Serve as vegetarian main dish.

Preparation / Cooking Tips: Use ricotta cheese in place of feta if not available.

Grilled Veggies

Preparation Time: 30 minutes
Cooking Time: 10 minutes
Servings: 4

Ingredients:

- 1 onion, sliced
- 1 red bell pepper, sliced
- 1 cup button mushrooms, sliced
- 1 zucchini, sliced
- 1 eggplant, sliced
- 1 cup asparagus, trimmed and sliced
- 1 squash, sliced
- 2 tablespoons olive oil
- Salt and pepper to taste

Method:

1. Install grill grate to your Ninja Foodi Grill.
2. Select grill setting.
3. Preheat it to medium for 10 minutes.
4. Toss the veggies in olive oil and season with salt and pepper.
5. Add to the grill grate.
6. Grill for 10 minutes.

Serving Suggestions: Sprinkle with dried herbs before serving.

Preparation / Cooking Tips: It's better to serve this dish at room temperature.

Asian Bok Choy

Preparation Time: 10 minutes
Cooking Time: 10 minutes
Servings: 4

Ingredients:

- 4 cups bok choy
- 2 tablespoons peanut oil
- 1 tablespoon oyster sauce
- 2 teaspoons garlic, minced
- Salt to taste

Method:

1. Coat bok choy with oil and oyster sauce.
2. Sprinkle with minced garlic and salt.
3. Add grill grate to your Ninja Foodi Grill.
4. Add bok choy on top of the grill.
5. Select grill setting. Set it to medium.
6. Grill for 10 minutes.

Serving Suggestions: Serve with peanut sauce on the side.

Preparation / Cooking Tips: You can also use Chinese cabbage for this recipe.

Vegetarian Bowl

Preparation Time: 20 minutes
Cooking Time: 25 minutes
Servings: 4

Ingredients:

- 3 cups tofu, sliced into cubes
- 1 cup red bell pepper, sliced into strips
- 1 cup yellow bell pepper, sliced into strips
- 1 cup mushroom, sliced
- 1/4 white onion, chopped
- Cooking spray
- Garlic salt to taste
- 4 cups cooked brown rice

Method:

1. Select air fry setting in your Ninja Foodi Grill.
2. Spray tofu cubes with oil.
3. Add tofu cubes to the air fryer basket.
4. Cook at 390 degrees F for 10 to 15 minutes or until crispy.
5. Transfer to a plate.
6. Toss veggies in a bowl.
7. Spray with oil and season with garlic salt.
8. Cook at 390 degrees F for 10 minutes, shaking the basket halfway through
9. Add brown rice to serving bowls.
10. Top with the crispy tofu and vegetables.

Serving Suggestions: Sprinkle with chopped scallions before serving.

Preparation / Cooking Tips: You can also use meat in lieu of tofu for this recipe if you prefer.

Mediterranean Veggies

Preparation Time: 30 minutes
Cooking Time: 20 minutes
Servings: 6

Ingredients:

- 1 zucchini, sliced
- 2 tomatoes, sliced in half
- 1 red bell pepper, sliced
- 1 orange bell pepper, sliced
- 1 yellow bell pepper, sliced
- 3 oz. black olives
- 1 tablespoon olive oil
- 1 teaspoon dried parsley
- 1 teaspoon dried oregano
- 1 teaspoon dried basil leaves
- Salt and pepper to taste
- 6 cloves garlic, minced

Method:

1. Combine all the ingredients in a large bowl.
2. Transfer to the air fryer basket.
3. Insert air fryer basket to your Ninja Foodi Grill.
4. Select air fry setting.
5. Cook at 390 degrees F for 10 minutes.
6. Stir and cook for another 10 minutes.

Serving Suggestions: Serve with crumbled feta cheese.

Preparation / Cooking Tips: Add other colorful veggies to this recipe.

Mexican Corn

Preparation Time: 15 minutes
Cooking Time: 10 minutes
Servings: 4

Ingredients:

- 4 ears corn
- 2 tablespoons oil
- Salt and pepper to taste
- 1/4 cup mayonnaise
- 1 cup Cotija cheese, crumbled
- 2 tablespoons lime juice
- 1/4 cup sour cream
- 1 teaspoon onion powder
- 1 teaspoon garlic powder

Method:

1. Install grill grate to your Ninja Foodi Grill.
2. Select grill function.
3. Set it to max for 12 minutes.
4. Press start to preheat.
5. Coat corn with oil.
6. Sprinkle all sides with salt and pepper.
7. Add corn to the grill.
8. Grill for 5 to 6 minutes.
9. Turn and cook for another 5 minutes.
10. Combine remaining ingredients in a bowl.
11. Coat the corn with the mixture and serve.

Serving Suggestions: Garnish with chopped cilantro.

Preparation / Cooking Tips: Use light mayonnaise and reduced-fat sour cream.

Vegetarian Pizza

Preparation Time: 20 minutes
Cooking Time: 15 minutes
Servings: 2

Ingredients:

- 1 pizza dough
- 1 tablespoon olive oil, divided
- 1/2 cup pizza sauce
- 1 cup mozzarella cheese, shredded
- 1/2 cup ricotta cheese
- 2 tomatoes, sliced
- 5 basil leaves, sliced

Method:

1. Add grill grate to the Ninja Foodi Grill.
2. Press grill setting.
3. Set it to max for 6 minutes.
4. Press start to preheat.
5. Roll out the dough on your kitchen table.
6. Brush top with oil.
7. Add dough to the grill.
8. Cook for 5 minutes.
9. Flip and cook for another 5 minutes.
10. Spread pizza sauce on top of the dough.
11. Sprinkle it with mozzarella cheese and then with ricotta.
12. Add tomatoes and basil on top.
13. Grill pizza for 3 to 5 minutes or until cheese has melted.

Serving Suggestions: Sprinkle with dried oregano before serving.

Preparation / Cooking Tips: Poke dough with fork before spreading with oil.

Roasted Cauliflower

Preparation Time: 30 minutes
Cooking Time: 20 minutes
Servings: 4

Ingredients:

- 2 heads cauliflower, sliced into florets
- 3 tablespoons olive oil
- Salt and pepper to taste

Sauce

- 1 tablespoon soy sauce
- 1/4 cup olive oil
- 1 tablespoon chili paste
- 3 tablespoons honey
- 2 tablespoons rice wine vinegar
- 1/4 cup roasted peanuts, chopped
- 1 tablespoon cilantro, chopped

Method:

1. Add air fry basket to your Ninja Foodi Grill.
2. Choose air fry function.
3. Set it to 390 degrees F for 20 minutes.
4. Press "start" to preheat.
5. In a bowl, toss cauliflower in oil.
6. Season with salt and pepper.
7. Add cauliflower to the air fry basket.
8. Seal the hood.
9. Cook for 10 minutes.
10. Stir and cook for another 8 minutes.
11. While waiting, combine all ingredients for sauce.
12. Toss the roasted cauliflower in sauce before serving.

Serving Suggestions: Garnish with sesame seeds.

Preparation / Cooking Tips: Use different colored cauliflower for a vibrant result.

Garlic Brussels Sprouts

Preparation Time: 15 minutes
Cooking Time: 35 minutes
Servings: 4

Ingredients:

- 1 lb. Brussels sprouts, sliced in half
- 1 tablespoon olive oil
- Salt and pepper to taste
- 2 teaspoons garlic powder

Method:

1. Toss Brussels sprouts in oil.
2. Season with salt, pepper and garlic powder.
3. Add crisper plate in the air fryer basket.
4. Add the basket to the Ninja Foodi Grill.
5. Select air fry. Set it to 390 degrees F for 3 minutes.
6. Press start to preheat.
7. Add Brussels sprouts to the crisper plate.
8. Cook for 20 minutes.
9. Stir and cook for another 15 minutes.

Serving Suggestions: Sprinkle with minced garlic on top if desired.

Preparation / Cooking Tips: Do not overcrowd the crisper plate to ensure even cooking.

Honey Carrots

Preparation Time: 15 minutes
Cooking Time: 10 minutes
Servings: 4

Ingredients:

- 2 tablespoons butter, melted
- 1 tablespoon honey
- Salt to taste
- 6 carrots, sliced
- 1 tablespoon parsley, chopped

Method:

1. Add grill grate to your Ninja Foodi Grill.
2. Set it to grill.
3. Press max temperature and set it to 10 minutes.
4. Choose start to preheat.
5. While preheating, combine butter, honey and salt.
6. Coat the carrots with the honey mixture.
7. Add carrots to the grill.
8. Seal the hood. Cook for 4 to 5 minutes.
9. Flip and cook for another 5 minutes.
10. Sprinkle with parsley and serve.

Serving Suggestions: Serve as side dish to a grilled meat dish.

Preparation / Cooking Tips: You can also add honey mixture after cooking.

Veggie Lasagna

Preparation Time: 30 minutes
Cooking Time: 45 minutes
Servings: 8

Ingredients:

- 6 cups tomato sauce
- 2 tablespoons olive oil
- 2 cloves garlic, minced
- 1 teaspoon dried basil
- 1 teaspoon dried oregano
- Salt and pepper to taste
- 1 red bell pepper, chopped
- 1 green bell pepper, chopped
- 1 cup mushrooms, diced
- 1 cup broccoli, diced
- 1 eggplant, diced
- 4 cups mozzarella cheese
- 4 cups cream
- 1 pack lasagna pasta sheets

Method:

1. Combine all ingredients except cheese, cream and pasta sheets.
2. In another bowl, mix cheese and cream.
3. Spread some of the tomato sauce and veggie mixture on the bottom of the pot.
4. Top with the pasta sheets.
5. Spread another layer of the tomato sauce mixture, and then the cheese mixture.
6. Top with another layer of pasta sheets.
7. Repeat layers until all ingredients have been used.
8. Cover the top layer with foil.
9. Choose bake setting.
10. Cook at 350 degrees F for 45 minutes.

Serving Suggestions: Sprinkle with Parmesan and basil before serving.

Preparation / Cooking Tips: You can also pre-boil the lasagna sheets and vegetables to reduce cooking time in the Ninja Foodi Grill.

Mixed Air Fried Veggies

Preparation Time: 20 minutes
Cooking Time: 20 minutes
Servings: 4

Ingredients:

- 1 white onion, sliced into wedges
- 1 red bell pepper, sliced
- 4 oz. mushroom buttons, sliced in half
- 1 zucchini, sliced
- 1 squash, sliced into cubes
- 1 tablespoon olive oil
- Salt and pepper to taste

Method:

1. Select air fry setting in your Ninja Foodi Grill.
2. Add air fryer basket.
3. Toss veggies in oil and season with salt and pepper.
4. Add veggies to the basket.
5. Cook for 10 minutes.
6. Shake and cook for another 10 minutes.

Serving Suggestions: Serve as side dish to a main course.

Preparation / Cooking Tips: You can also try using other vegetables for this recipe like potatoes or carrots.

Chapter 8: Snack and Appetizer

Parmesan French Fries

Preparation Time: 15 minutes
Cooking Time: 15 minutes
Servings: 6

Ingredients:

- 1 lb. French fries
- 1/2 cup mayonnaise
- 2 cloves garlic, minced
- 1 tablespoon oil
- Salt and pepper to taste
- 1 teaspoon garlic powder
- 1/2 cup Parmesan cheese, grated
- 1 teaspoon lemon juice

Method:

1. Add crisper basket to your Ninja Foodi Grill.
2. Select air fry function.
3. Set it to 375 degrees F for 22 minutes.
4. Press start to preheat.
5. Add fries to the basket.
6. Cook for 10 minutes.
7. Shake and cook for another 5 minutes.
8. Toss in oil and sprinkle with Parmesan cheese.
9. Mix the remaining ingredients in a bowl.
10. Serve fries with this sauce.

Serving Suggestions: Sprinkle chopped parsley and serve.

Preparation / Cooking Tips: Buy frozen fries for convenience.

Peanut Butter & Banana Snacks

Preparation Time: 15 minutes
Cooking Time: 10 minutes
Servings: 4

Ingredients:

- 1 cup peanut butter
- 8 slices whole wheat bread
- 1 cup jam
- 2 bananas, sliced
- 2 teaspoons ground cinnamon
- 1/4 cup white sugar
- Cooking spray

Method:

1. Spread peanut butter on 4 bread slices.
2. Spread jam on the remaining bread slices.
3. Add bananas and make 4 sandwiches.
4. In a bowl, mix cinnamon and sugar.
5. Select air fry function in your Ninja Foodi Grill.
6. Set it to 390 degrees F for 3 minutes.
7. Add crisper plate to the air fryer basket.
8. Spray sandwiches with oil and sprinkle with cinnamon mixture.
9. Air fry sandwiches for 6 minutes.
10. Flip and cook for 3 more minutes.

Serving Suggestions: Serve with chocolate hazelnut spread.

Preparation / Cooking Tips: Use creamy peanut butter for this recipe.

Homemade Fries

Preparation Time: 15 minutes
Cooking Time: 45 minutes
Servings: 6

Ingredients:

- 1 lb. large potatoes, sliced into strips
- 2 tablespoons vegetable oil
- Salt to taste

Method:

1. Toss potato strips in oil.
2. Add crisper plate to the air fryer basket inside the Ninja Foodi Grill.
3. Choose air fry function. Set it to 390 degrees F for 3 minutes.
4. Press start to preheat.
5. Add potato strips to the crisper plate.
6. Cook for 25 minutes.
7. Stir and cook for another 20 minutes.

Serving Suggestions: Serve with ketchup and mayo.

Preparation / Cooking Tips: Soak potato strips in cold water for 30 minutes before cooking.

Bacon Bell Peppers

Preparation Time: 10 minutes
Cooking Time: 5 minutes
Servings: 16

Ingredients:

- 1 pack bacon slices
- 12 bell peppers, sliced in half
- 8 oz. cream cheese

Method:

1. Stuff bell pepper halves with cream cheese.
2. Wrap with bacon slices.
3. Preheat Ninja Foodi Grill to 500 degrees F.
4. Add bell peppers to the grill.
5. Grill for 3 to 5 minutes.

Serving Suggestions: Sprinkle with chopped parsley before serving.

Preparation / Cooking Tips: You can use toothpicks to secure bacon and simply remove these before serving.

Fried Garlic Pickles

Preparation Time: 20 minutes
Cooking Time: 15 minutes
Servings: 6

Ingredients:

- 1/4 cup all-purpose flour
- Pinch baking powder
- 2 tablespoons water
- Salt to taste
- 20 dill pickle slices
- 2 tablespoons cornstarch
- 1 1/2 cups panko bread crumbs
- 2 teaspoons garlic powder
- 2 tablespoons canola oil

Method:

1. In a bowl, combine flour, baking powder, water and salt.
2. Add more water if batter is too thick.
3. Put the cornstarch in a second bowl, and mix breadcrumbs and garlic powder in a third bowl.
4. Dip pickles in cornstarch, then in the batter and finally dredge with breadcrumb mixture.
5. Add crisper plate to the air fryer basket inside the Ninja Foodi Grill.
6. Press air fry setting.
7. Set it to 360 degrees F for 3 minutes.
8. Press start to preheat.
9. Add pickles to the crisper plate.
10. Brush with oil.
11. Air fry for 10 minutes.
12. Flip, brush with oil and cook for another 5 minutes.

Serving Suggestions: Serve with ketchup or sweet chili sauce.

Preparation / Cooking Tips: Dry pickles before coating with breading.

Zucchini Strips with Marinara Dip

Preparation Time: 1 hour and 10 minutes
Cooking Time: 30 minutes
Servings: 8

Ingredients:

- 2 zucchinis, sliced into strips
- Salt to taste
- 1 1/2 cups all-purpose flour
- 2 eggs, beaten
- 2 cups bread crumbs
- 2 teaspoons onion powder
- 1 tablespoon garlic powder
- 1/4 cup Parmesan cheese, grated
- 1/2 cup marinara sauce

Method:

1. Season zucchini with salt.
2. Let sit for 15 minutes.
3. Pat dry with paper towels.
4. Add flour to a bowl.
5. Add eggs to another bowl.
6. Mix remaining ingredients except marinara sauce in a third bowl.
7. Dip zucchini strips in the first, second and third bowls.
8. Cover with foil and freeze for 45 minutes.
9. Add crisper plate to the air fryer basket inside the Ninja Foodi Grill.
10. Select air fry function.
11. Preheat to 360 degrees F for 3 minutes.
12. Add zucchini strips to the crisper plate.
13. Air fry for 20 minutes.
14. Flip and cook for another 10 minutes.
15. Serve with marinara dip.

Serving Suggestions: Serve with side salad.

Preparation / Cooking Tips: Use reduced-sodium marinara sauce as dip.

Crunchy Parmesan Asparagus

Preparation Time: 10 minutes
Cooking Time: 10 minutes
Servings: 4

Ingredients:

- 1/4 cup all-purpose flour
- Salt to taste
- 2 eggs, beaten
- 1/4 cup Parmesan cheese, grated
- 1/2 cup breadcrumbs
- 1 cup asparagus, trimmed
- Cooking spray

Method:

1. Mix flour and salt in a bowl.
2. Add eggs to a second bowl.
3. Combine Parmesan cheese and breadcrumbs in a third bowl.
4. Dip asparagus spears in the first, second and third bowls.
5. Spray with oil.
6. Add crisper plate to the air fryer basket inside the Ninja Foodi Grill.
7. Set it to air fry.
8. Preheat at 390 degrees F for 3 minutes.
9. Add asparagus to the plate.
10. Air fry for 5 minutes per side.

Serving Suggestions: Serve with ranch dressing as dip.

Preparation / Cooking Tips: Dry asparagus thoroughly before breading.

Bacon & Sausages

Preparation Time: 10 minutes
Cooking Time: 20 minutes
Servings: 4

Ingredients:

- 4 sausages
- 8 bacon slices

Method:

1. Add crisper plate to the air fryer basket inside the Ninja Foodi Grill.
2. Press air fry setting.
3. Preheat at 360 degrees F for 3 minutes.
4. Wrap 2 bacon slices around each sausage.
5. Add these to the crisper plate.
6. Cook for 10 minutes per side.

Serving Suggestions: Serve with ketchup and mustard.

Preparation / Cooking Tips: Use Italian sausage for this recipe.

Crispy Pickles

Preparation Time: 15 minutes
Cooking Time: 30 minutes
Servings: 4

Ingredients:

- 1 cup all-purpose flour
- 3 eggs
- 1 cup breadcrumbs
- Garlic salt to taste
- 12 dill pickle spears
- Cooking spray

Method:

1. Dip pickles in flour, eggs and then in a mixture of breadcrumbs and garlic salt.
2. Arrange on a plate.
3. Place inside the freezer for 30 minutes.
4. Add crisper basket to the Ninja Foodi Grill.
5. Choose air fry function.
6. Add pickles to the basket.
7. Spray with oil.
8. Cook at 375 degrees F for 18 to 20 minutes.
9. Flip and cook for another 10 minutes.

Serving Suggestions: Mix mayo, mustard and ketchup. Serve with fried pickles.

Preparation / Cooking Tips: Pat the pickles dry with paper towel before breading.

Sweet Potato Wedges

Preparation Time: 10 minutes
Cooking Time: 20 minutes
Servings: 4

Ingredients:

- 2 sweet potatoes, sliced into wedges
- 1 tablespoon vegetable oil
- 1 teaspoon smoked paprika
- 1 tablespoon honey
- Salt and pepper to taste

Method:

1. Add air fryer basket to your Ninja Foodi Grill.
2. Choose air fry setting.
3. Preheat at 390 degrees for 25 minutes.
4. Add sweet potato wedges to the basket.
5. Cook for 10 minutes.
6. Stir and cook for another 10 minutes.
7. Toss in paprika and honey.
8. Sprinkle with salt and pepper.

Serving Suggestions: Serve with your preferred dipping sauce.

Preparation / Cooking Tips: Soak sweet potato wedges in cold water for 30 minutes, and then drain and pat dry before seasoning.

Fish Sticks

Preparation Time: 15 minutes
Cooking Time: 15 minutes
Servings: 8

Ingredients:

- 16 oz. tilapia fillets, sliced into strips
- 1 cup all-purpose flour
- 2 eggs
- 1 1/2 cups breadcrumbs
- Salt to taste

Method:

1. Dip fish strips in flour and then in eggs.
2. Mix breadcrumbs and salt.
3. Coat fish strips with breadcrumbs.
4. Add fish strips to a crisper plate.
5. Place crisper plate inside the basket.
6. Choose air fry setting.
7. Cook fish strips at 390 degrees F for 12 to 15 minutes, flipping once halfway through.

Serving Suggestions: Serve with tartar sauce and ketchup.

Preparation / Cooking Tips: You can use other types of white fish for this recipe.

Ranch Chicken Fingers

Preparation Time: 15 minutes
Cooking Time: 20 minutes
Servings: 4

Ingredients:

- 2 lb. chicken breast fillet, sliced into strips
- 1 tablespoon olive oil
- 1 oz. ranch dressing seasoning mix
- 4 cups breadcrumbs
- Salt to taste

Method:

1. Coat chicken strips with olive oil.
2. Sprinkle all sides with ranch seasoning.
3. Cover with foil and refrigerate for 1 to 2 hours.
4. In a bowl, mix breadcrumbs and salt.
5. Dredge the chicken strips with seasoned breadcrumbs.
6. Add crisper plate to the air fryer basket inside the Ninja Foodi Grill.
7. Choose air fry setting.
8. Set it to 390 degrees F.
9. Preheat for 3 minutes.
10. Add chicken strips to the crisper plate.
11. Cook for 15 to 20 minutes, flipping halfway through.

Serving Suggestions: Serve with ketchup and mayo.

Preparation / Cooking Tips: Arrange chicken strips on the crisper plate on a single layer.

Grilled Tomato Salsa

Preparation Time: 15 minutes
Cooking Time: 10 minutes
Servings: 4 to 8

Ingredients:

- 1 onion, sliced
- 1 jalapeño pepper, sliced in half
- 5 tomatoes, sliced
- 2 tablespoons oil
- Salt and pepper to taste
- 1 cup cilantro, trimmed and sliced
- 1 tablespoon lime juice
- 1 teaspoon lime zest
- 2 tablespoons ground cumin
- 3 cloves garlic, peeled and sliced

Method:

1. Coat onion, jalapeño pepper and tomatoes with oil.
2. Season with salt and pepper.
3. Add grill grate to your Ninja Foodi Grill.
4. Press grill setting.
5. Choose max temperature and set it to 10 minutes.
6. Press start to preheat.
7. Add vegetables on the grill.
8. Cook for 5 minutes per side.
9. Transfer to a plate and let cool.
10. Add vegetable mixture to a food processor.
11. Stir in remaining ingredients.
12. Pulse until smooth.

Serving Suggestions: Serve with nacho chips.

Preparation / Cooking Tips: You can also add chili powder to the food processor if you want your salsa spicy.

Greek Potatoes

Preparation Time: 20 minutes
Cooking Time: 30 minutes
Servings: 4

Ingredients:

- 1 lb. potatoes, sliced into wedges
- 2 tablespoons olive oil
- 1 teaspoon paprika
- 2 teaspoons dried oregano
- Salt and pepper to taste
- 1/4 cup onion, diced
- 2 tablespoons lemon juice
- 1 tomato, diced
- 1/4 cup black olives, sliced
- 1/2 cup feta cheese, crumbled

Method:

1. Add crisper plate to the air fryer basket inside the Ninja Foodi Grill.
2. Choose air fry setting.
3. Set it to 390 degrees F.
4. Preheat for 3 minutes.
5. While preheating, toss potatoes in oil.
6. Sprinkle with paprika, oregano, salt and pepper.
7. Add potatoes to the crisper plate.
8. Air fry for 18 minutes.
9. Toss and cook for another 5 minutes.
10. Add onion and cook for 5 minutes.
11. Transfer to a bowl.
12. Stir in the rest of the ingredients.

Serving Suggestions: Garnish with fresh dill.

Preparation / Cooking Tips: Use freshly squeezed lemon juice.

Garlic Parmesan Fries

Preparation Time: 15 minutes
Cooking Time: 20 minutes
Servings: 4

Ingredients:

- 3 potatoes, sliced into sticks
- 2 tablespoons vegetable oil, divided
- 1/4 cup Parmesan cheese, grated
- 2 cloves garlic, minced
- 1 teaspoon garlic powder
- Salt to taste

Method:

1. Coat potato strips with half of oil.
2. Add crisper plate to the air fryer basket inside the Ninja Foodi Grill.
3. Select air fry function.
4. Preheat at 360 degrees F for 3 minutes.
5. Add fries to the crisper plate
6. Cook for 12 minutes.
7. Flip and cook for another 5 minutes.
8. Combine remaining ingredients in a bowl.
9. Toss fries in the mixture and serve.

Serving Suggestions: Sprinkle with chopped parsley before serving.

Preparation / Cooking Tips: Use russet potatoes for this recipe.

Chapter 9: Desserts

Strawberry & Cake Kebabs

Preparation Time: 15 minutes
Cooking Time: 6 minutes
Servings: 5

Ingredients:

- 1 pack white cake mix
- 2 cups strawberries, sliced in half
- 2 tablespoons honey
- 1/4 cup sugar
- Cooking spray

Method:

1. Cook cake mix according to the directions in the box.
2. Insert the grill grate in the Ninja Foodi Grill.
3. Choose grill setting.
4. Preheat at 325 degrees F for 15 minutes.
5. While waiting, slice cake into cubes.
6. Toss strawberries in honey and sugar.
7. Thread cake cubes and strawberries alternately onto skewers.
8. Grill for 3 minutes per side.

Serving Suggestions: Serve with vanilla ice cream.

Preparation / Cooking Tips: When preparing cake mix, you can replace water with pudding to make the cake thicker.

Fudge Brownies

Preparation Time: 20 minutes
Cooking Time: 1 hour
Servings: 6

Ingredients:

- 1/2 cup all-purpose flour
- Pinch salt
- 1/4 cup cocoa powder
- 2 eggs
- 1/2 cup brown sugar
- 1/2 cup white sugar
- 1 tablespoon vanilla extract
- 1 tablespoon water
- 3/4 cup butter, melted
- 6 oz. chocolate chips, melted

Method:

1. Combine flour, salt and cocoa powder in a bowl.
2. Beat eggs in another bowl.
3. Stir in sugars, vanilla and water.
4. Add butter and chocolate chips to the mixture.
5. Slowly add dry ingredients to this mixture.
6. Mix well.
7. Spray small baking pan with oil.
8. Pour batter into the pan.
9. Add crisper plate to the air fry basket in the Ninja Foodi Grill.
10. Choose air fry setting.
11. Preheat at 300 degrees F for 3 minutes.
12. Add small baking pan to the crisper plate.
13. Cook for 1 hour.

Serving Suggestions: Serve with milk.

Preparation / Cooking Tips: Use unsweetened cocoa powder.

Cinnamon Apple Chips

Preparation Time: 10 minutes
Cooking Time: 12 minutes
Servings: 4

Ingredients:

- 1 apple, sliced thinly
- 2 teaspoons vegetable oil
- 1 teaspoon ground cinnamon
- Cooking spray

Method:

1. Coat the apples slices in oil and sprinkle with cinnamon.
2. Spray the air fryer basket with oil.
3. Choose air fry setting in the Ninja Foodi Grill.
4. Air fry the apples at 375 degrees F for 12 minutes, flipping once or twice.

Serving Suggestions: Serve with almond yogurt dip.

Preparation / Cooking Tips: Use a mandolin to slice the apples very thinly.

Grilled Donuts

Preparation Time: 15 minutes
Cooking Time: 10 minutes
Servings: 8

Ingredients:

- 1/4 cup milk
- 1 teaspoon vanilla extract
- 2 cups powdered sugar
- 16 oz. prepared biscuit dough
- Cooking spray

Method:

1. In a bowl, mix milk, vanilla and sugar.
2. Cut rings from the prepared dough.
3. Refrigerate for 5 minutes.
4. Add grill grate to the Ninja Foodi Grill.
5. Choose grill setting.
6. Set it to medium
7. Preheat for 6 minutes.
8. Spray round dough with oil.
9. Add to the grill and cook for 4 minutes.
10. Dip in the milk mixture and grill for another 4 minutes.

Serving Suggestions: Sprinkle with cinnamon sugar or chocolate sprinkles before serving.

Strawberry Pop Tarts

Preparation Time: 20 minutes
Cooking Time: 20 minutes
Servings: 6

Ingredients:

- 8 oz. strawberries
- 1/4 cup granulated sugar
- 1 refrigerated pie crust
- Cooking spray

Method:

1. Combine strawberries and sugar in a pan over medium heat.
2. Cook while stirring for 10 minutes.
3. Let cool.
4. Spread pie crust on your kitchen table.
5. Slice into rectangles.
6. Add strawberries on top of the rectangles.
7. Brush edges with water.
8. Wrap and seal.
9. Spray tarts with oil.
10. Add tarts to the air fryer basket.
11. Choose air fry setting in your Ninja Foodi Grill.
12. Air fry at 350 degrees F for 10 minutes.
13. Let cool before serving.

Serving Suggestions: Sprinkle with colorful candy sprinkles before serving.

Preparation / Cooking Tips: You can also use other berries for this recipe.

Peanut Butter Cups

Preparation Time: 5 minutes
Cooking Time: 5 minutes
Servings: 4

Ingredients:

- 4 graham crackers
- 4 peanut butter cups
- 4 marshmallows

Method:

1. Add crisper plate to the air fryer basket of your Ninja Foodi Grill.
2. Choose air fry function.
3. Preheat at 360 degrees F for 3 minutes.
4. Break the crackers in half.
5. Add crackers to the crisper plate.
6. Top with the peanut butter cups.
7. Cook for 2 minutes.
8. Sprinkle mushrooms on top and cook for another 1 minute.
9. Top with the remaining crackers and serve.

Serving Suggestions: Serve with warm milk.

Preparation / Cooking Tips: You can also use chocolate spread in place of peanut butter cups if you like.

Cookies

Preparation Time: 10 minutes
Cooking Time: 10 minutes
Servings: 2

Ingredients:

- 4 oz. cookie dough

Method:

1. Choose air fry setting in your Ninja Foodi Grill.
2. Set it to 350 degrees F.
3. Preheat it for 1 minute.
4. Line air fryer basket with parchment paper.
5. Create 6 cookies from the dough.
6. Add these to the air fryer basket.
7. Place air fryer basket inside the unit.
8. Cook for 8 to 10 minutes.

Serving Suggestions: Serve with warm milk.

Preparation / Cooking Tips: Make sure there is enough space between the cookies.

Grilled Apple Pie

Preparation Time: 30 minutes
Cooking Time: 30 minutes
Servings: 8

Ingredients:

- 8 cups cold water
- 1 tablespoon lemon juice
- 8 apples, diced
- 1/2 cup brown sugar
- 1/2 teaspoon ground cinnamon
- 1/2 teaspoon ground ginger
- 3 tablespoons all-purpose flour
- 1/2 cup applesauce
- 1 frozen pie crust

Method:

1. In a bowl, mix water, lemon juice and apples.
2. Let sit for 10 minutes.
3. Drain and pat dry.
4. Add grill grate to Ninja Foodi Grill.
5. Press grill setting.
6. Set it to max and preheat for 8 minutes.
7. Coat apples with sugar.
8. Grill for 8 minutes without flipping.
9. In a bowl, combine the remaining ingredients.
10. Stir in grilled apples.
11. Pour the mixture into a small baking pan.
12. Top with the pie crust.
13. Select bake setting.
14. Cook pie at 350 degrees F for 20 minutes.

Serving Suggestions: Serve with vanilla ice cream.

Preparation / Cooking Tips: Defrost pie crust before using.

Fried Oreos

Preparation Time: 10 minutes
Cooking Time: 5 minutes
Servings: 8

Ingredients:

- 8 oz. crescent rolls (refrigerated)
- 16 Oreos
- 3 tablespoons peanut butter

Method:

1. Spread dough onto a working surface.
2. Slice into 8 rectangles.
3. Slice each rectangle into 2.
4. Add cookie on top of the dough.
5. Spread with peanut butter.
6. Wrap the dough around the Oreos.
7. Place these in the air fryer basket inside the Ninja Foodi Grill.
8. Choose air fry setting.
9. Air fry at 320 degrees F for 5 minutes.

Serving Suggestions: Dust with powdered sugar before serving.

Preparation / Cooking Tips: You can also use this recipe for other sandwich cookies.

Baked Apples

Preparation Time: 15 minutes
Cooking Time: 45 minutes
Servings: 4

Ingredients:

- 2 apples, sliced in half
- 1 tablespoon lemon juice
- 4 teaspoons brown sugar
- 1/4 cup butter, sliced into small cubes

Method:

1. Add crisper plate to the air fryer basket inside the Ninja Foodi Grill.
2. Choose air fry function.
3. Preheat it to 325 degrees F for 3 minutes.
4. Add apples to the crisper plate.
5. Drizzle with lemon juice and sprinkle with brown sugar.
6. Place butter cubes on top.
7. Air fry for 45 minutes.

Serving Suggestions: Top with caramel syrup or crushed graham crackers.

Preparation / Cooking Tips: Poke apples with a fork before cooking.

Chapter 10: 30-Day Meal Plan

Day 1

Breakfast: Spicy sausage and mushroom casserole

Lunch: Sugar glazed chicken

Dinner: Grilled herbed steak

Day 2

Breakfast: Honey carrots

Lunch: Tenderloin steak with bacon

Dinner: Grilled citrus fish

Day 3

Breakfast: Breakfast potatoes

Lunch: Lemon garlic chicken

Dinner: Paprika pork chops

Day 4

Breakfast: Mexican corn

Lunch: Shrimp bang bang

Dinner: Roasted chicken

Day 5

Breakfast: French toast

Lunch: Ranch pork chops

Dinner: Roasted cauliflower

Day 6

Breakfast: Eggs and avocado

Lunch: Chicken, potatoes and cabbage

Dinner: Herbed salmon

Day 7

Breakfast: Breakfast omelet

Lunch: Teriyaki salmon

Dinner: Roast beef and grilled potatoes

Day 8

Breakfast: Ham and cheese casserole

Lunch: Roasted mixed veggies

Dinner: Shrimp fajitas

Day 9

Breakfast: Breakfast casserole

Lunch: Barbeque chicken breast

Dinner: Cuban pork chops

Day 10

Breakfast: Garlic Brussels sprouts

Lunch: Crispy fish fillet

Dinner: Vegetarian pizza

Day 11

Breakfast: Breakfast bell peppers

Lunch: Chicken and zucchini

Dinner: Steak kebab

Day 12

Breakfast: Mediterranean veggies and quinoa

Lunch: Grilled ranch chicken

Dinner: Herbed salmon

Day 13

Breakfast: Breakfast burrito

Lunch: Crispy fish sandwich

Dinner: Grilled pork chops

Day 14

Breakfast: Eggs and avocado

Lunch: Crumbed flounder fillet

Dinner: Roasted beef with garlic

Day 15

Breakfast: Roasted spicy potatoes

Lunch: Chicken quesadilla

Dinner: Grilled lemon pepper shrimp

Day 16

Breakfast: French toast sticks

Lunch: Roast beef with garlic

Dinner: Veggie lasagna

Day 17

Breakfast: Roasted breakfast potatoes

Lunch: Grilled cauliflower steak

Dinner: Salmon with coconut aminos

Day 18

Breakfast: Eggs and avocado

Lunch: Beer battered cod

Dinner: Coffee ribeye

Day 19

Breakfast: Mixed air fried veggies

Lunch: Sausage and pepper

Dinner: Buffalo chicken wings

Day 20

Breakfast: Crispy garlic potatoes

Lunch: Grilled paprika salmon

Dinner: Grilled herbed steak

Day 21

Breakfast: Bacon

Lunch: Vegetarian bowl

Dinner: Grilled steak and potatoes

Day 22

Breakfast: Spicy sausage and mushroom casserole

Lunch: Fried chicken

Dinner: Honey garlic shrimp

Day 23

Breakfast: Sausage casserole

Lunch: Grilled shrimp

Dinner: Grilled balsamic chicken breast

Day 24

Breakfast: Breakfast burrito

Lunch: Steak with asparagus

Dinner: Mustard chicken

Day 25

Breakfast: French toast sticks

Lunch: Grilled garlic chicken

Dinner: Asian bok choy

Day 26

Breakfast: Breakfast casserole

Lunch: Crispy fish sandwich

Dinner: Ribeye steak with onions and peppers

Day 27

Breakfast: Eggs and avocado

Lunch: Cheeseburger

Dinner: Cuban pork chops

Day 28

Breakfast: Mediterranean veggies and quinoa

Lunch: Honey and rosemary chicken

Dinner: Herbed salmon

Day 29

Breakfast: Mexican corn

Lunch: Shrimp boil

Dinner: Steak kebab

Day 30

Breakfast: Hash browns

Lunch: Grilled chicken with veggies

Dinner: Coffee ribeye

Conclusion

The Mediterranean Ninja Foodi Grill Cookbook for Beginners is specially designed for combining the Ninja Foodi Grill with Mediterranean diet. This book contains many delicious recipes commonly used in the Mediterranean style. We provide accurate Preparation Time, Cooking Time, Service, Ingredients, Preparation, Nutrition and other information for each recipe, making your cooking easier and faster. This book is perfect for a Ninja Foodi Grill. This is also to satisfy all your Grill needs.

Thank you for buying this book. Now let's start your gourmet journey!

CPSIA information can be obtained
at www.ICGtesting.com
Printed in the USA
BVHW050851150621
609531BV00007B/2113